Global Education

School-based Strategies

GLOBAL

EDUCATION

School-based Strategies

Edited by

Kenneth A. Tye

Interdependence Press
Orange, California

L C

1090

. G 551

1990

1 5 - 5 4 7 3

apr. 1992

ISBN 0-9626957-1-8

Interdependence Press
435 North Harwood
Orange, California 92666

Manufactured in the United States of America.

Acknowledgements

Appreciation is expressed to Leslie Adcock and John Trausch who assisted a great deal in the production of this book.

Contents

INTRODUCTION

John I. Goodlad

This book is remarkable in three ways. First, it simply assumes that "today's children will have to face complex issues such as arms control, environmental protection, food production and energy use." (This is taken from the first sentence of Chapter Four.) Even in the light of the very best scenarios of the future, the contents of this sentence are no longer subjects of debate. Just the other day, it seems, it was. Second, every chapter aligns with another theme that is central suddenly to educational reform and little debated: The school is the center of improvement. "Site-based management" and "site-based renewal" have become the rallying call for policymakers and teachers alike. Third, each chapter adds to and confirms fundamental principles of educational change, while eschewing theoretical discourse.

For several decades, a handful of educators—Charlotte and Lee Anderson, James Becker, Robert Freeman, Bruce Joyce, David King, Robert Leestma, Judith Torney, and Kenneth Tye (to name just several)—sustained the idea that our children must come to understand the degree to which we live in a global village. They pushed and prodded us to comprehend that the meaning of global must be added to our understanding of national and international. Sometimes, near-cataclysmic events are required to shake us loose from hardened categories to new ways of thinking. Recent events in China and Eastern Europe have served this purpose, advancing the ideas of these and other educators from the controversial to the near-incontrovertible. Although the words "global education" still stir alarm in many communities, the ensuing debate is now almost invariably over the religious issues that have arisen around these two words and not over whether children and youths in our schools should better comprehend the interconnectedness of the world around them.

And so, what were once the frontiers of educational thought and practice are increasingly being populated by legions of believers endeavoring to develop the curricula and modes of instruction required "to raise the level of awareness [among ALL] of the five world systems: ecological, cultural, economic, political, and technological" (from Chapter One). Those of us who have endeavored to assist principals and teachers with infusing a global perspective into classroom activities know how difficult this is. Although teachers today are surrounded with materials on countries and customs in addition to those on the United States, many of these fail dismally in regard to portraying, for example, the degree to which our economy is connected to a worldwide economic system. Those in schools and classrooms with whom I have worked would have been helped immeasurably by the experiences of others portrayed in the chapters that follow.

These accounts reveal that there is no *one* way to begin and proceed. Indeed, the genesis of each is quite different from that of the others. In several, successful projects began in ways that contradict research on change. But, in nearly all, the initiative began with one person or a small group of individuals, sometimes quite serendipitously. Increasingly, qualitative studies are revealing that lasting, evolving change begins at and grows from the grassroots—and usually because someone or several people resonated to the beat of an alternative drummer.

The stories are of schools that differ markedly. They are in ten different states; they are in rural, suburban, and urban settings; they vary widely in resources and in economic status of their students; and they represent the elementary and both middle and high school levels of schooling. Although new curricular requirements were occasionally the driving force, usually the beginnings were a kind of spontaneous reaction to a recognized need—a reaction reinforced and legitimated early on by a chance encounter outside the school, by a consultant, or at a workshop.

This is a book for the stewards of individual schools— principals, teachers, parents—and all those individuals who want to find ways to encourage these stewards to renew their schools. Yes, the pervasive theme is global education, but the processes of renewal portrayed are those increasingly found to be most productive of lasting change. Although the locus is the school, work is further decentralized to small task forces and sometimes to "schools-within-schools." The role of the principal in creating opportunities to integrate the pieces is critical. We come to see importance, too, of connections to a knowledge base and of renewing schools to one another.

These case studies possess the ring of authenticity that simply cannot be portrayed in the rhetoric of school reform. Not one sounds contrived; not one is boring; each carries a message that transcends the specifics of description. Read and enjoy.

CHAPTER ONE

SETTING THE STAGE

Kenneth A. Tye

Most Americans are becoming aware of the growing economic, ecological, technological and even political and cultural interdependence of today's world. They know something about such issues as trade imbalances and ozone depletion. They are even more cognizant of technological interconnectedness, as represented by rapid air travel, computer and satellite linkages, faxing, and the like. Recently, too, our media have been full of reports of political collaboration among nations in such areas as control of terrorism, the settlement of regional conflicts, and nuclear disarmament. Some people are even becoming aware of a growing cultural interdependence as worldwide migration patterns literally change the demographic makeup of local communities.

Even with obvious connections and collaborations, however, most of us do not tend to think of ourselves as living in an interdependent world, nor do our schools teach about such interdependence. John Goodlad has noted that most of the world's educational systems have as one of their goals developing understanding and appreciation of other nations, other cultures, other peoples. He states:

> ...Use of the word "other" is revealing. It connotes a "we-they" kind of thinking that pervades most countries and their educational systems...Such programs promote nationalism...The development of global perspectives...is not an established goal in any country...The meaning and significance of such a goal

can be described, at best, as only emerging. Gaining widespread
acceptance of it and implementing what it implies will not be
easy.[1]

Given the realities of today's world, schools can no
longer afford to promote this "we-they" kind of thinking.
They need to take the lead in developing positive attitudes in
children, youth, and adults toward human interdependence.
Initially, there is a need to raise the level of consciousness
about the ecological, cultural, economic, political and
technological systems of the world. The ultimate goal of
global education is to cause people to transcend more
limited levels of interest and to take personal and collective
action on behalf of all humankind.

In 1985, with a grant from the Helen Devitt Jones
Foundation, the Center for Human Interdependence (CHI) at
Chapman College in southern California was established to
(1) organize a network of elementary and secondary schools
in which a significant number of teachers would commit
themselves to the development of a global perspective, and
(2) study this development, in an attempt to answer the
question, "What does it take to bring a global perspective to
the curriculum of a school?" The story of the project is
partially told in this book in Chapters 5 and 9, in which
programs at Park View School and Tuffree Junior High are
described. In-depth reports are presented in other places.[2] It
is enough to state here that the criteria for inclusion of a
school in the CHI network were simply that (1) the
superintendent, principal, and a significant number of
teachers (purposely never precisely defined, but ranging
from 10-50 percent) had to agree to participate, and (2) each
district had to provide 10-15 days of teacher release time for
use by each school involved in the project.

Nothing was imposed upon the participants. Instead, the
project was begun by asking them what *they* were interested
in doing. CHI staff members visited the schools, providing
instructional materials, consultants, and ideas as the need for
such resources was identified by the school people: teachers,
administrators, and support personnel. Small grants

(approximately $600 each) were offered, no strings attached, to teachers and others who had ideas about how to globalize the curriculum. Proposals were judged by a panel composed of project participants and CHI staff members. Network-wide activities (workshops, conferences, special projects) were carried out which brought staff members from various schools together to work on common interests—e.g., workshops on global economics, folk art and folklore, environmental issues, conflict resolution, dealing with controversial issues. A newsletter which featured school activities, global education concepts, and practical lessons was published regularly. There were also some special projects involving segments of the network. Four schools had international telecommunications connections, middle school students came together from several schools for an international sports day at which non-competitive games from around the world were played, and volunteer teachers from several schools participated in an "Orange County in the World" project modeled after the "Columbus in the World" program developed by the Mershon Center at Ohio State University.[3]

The research employed qualitative field study methodologies in an effort to develop what Glaser and Strauss call "grounded theory."[4] Further, and while the project was not totally limited to one theoretical perspective, it was heavily influenced by Herbert Blumer and other Symbolic Interactionists.[5] Simply put, this implies that the focus of the study was the *meanings* which people gave to their experience.

Each CHI staff member kept careful field notes of every visit to any of the eleven participating schools. As these accumulated, they were grouped into observational notes (what actually happened), theoretical notes (what it might mean), and methodological notes (what CHI should try next, or do differently next time, etc.). Periodically, individual staff members prepared "memos" which pulled together a person's thinking about an emerging pattern or concept.

There were frequent research team meetings to discuss and reflect upon findings. Often a "memo" served as the beginning point of a discussion. The usual outcome of such a meeting was the raising of further questions which became the foci of subsequent observations and/or interviews. The process was one of data gathering, reflection, hypothesis generation, further data gathering, and so on.

An assumption which guided activities of the CHI network project was that change efforts are best focused at the school site level. Previous research by this author has shown that most teacher in-service education occurs individually and more or less idiosyncratically and, while it might affect the classroom performance of the teacher positively, it does not have any particular impact on school-level outcomes.[6] Further, despite all of the political rhetoric to the contrary, the "top-down" state mandates of the 80's have not really done much to improve schooling. The notion in preparing this case book was to return to the recommendations of the major reports on schooling resulting from change efforts in the 60's and 70's which were largely ignored in the 80's. These reports, the most notable authored individually by Boyer, Goodlad, and Sizer, all point to the school as the critical unit and suggest that improvement efforts be focused there.[7]

Further, and this is critical, they call for each school to be linked to some knowledge base such as, in this case, the Center for Human Interdependence.[8]

As work was begun with the network of schools, there was a natural curiosity about what other global education efforts were under way across the country. An examination found many, and the number growing. As of this writing, there are state mandates for one or two years of global studies as part of high school graduation requirements in Alaska, Arkansas, Georgia, Minnesota, New Jersey, New York, Vermont, and Wisconsin. In Hawaii, Indiana, Tennessee and Utah, state social studies frameworks and/or curriculum guides have been revised to include global education strands. In Florida, Virginia, and Washington, state advisory boards and/or offices of international education have been established, with state grants made available to school districts. Legislatures have funded statewide satellite global education centers in California and Massachusetts. Even where there is no specific mandate for global and/or international studies, there is often a statewide increase in social studies requirements which, in turn, make way for the addition of global education to the curriculum.

As laudable as such mandates are, they, by themselves, do not guarantee that the curricula of schools will take on a global perspective. As was previously noted, the single school is the critical unit of change and improvement efforts need to be focused there.

When many of the efforts across the country to globalize curricula were examined, it was pleasantly surprising to note the large number which, explicitly or implicitly, operated from assumptions similar to CHI's about the importance of a school-based focus and the linkage of the school to a knowledge base. It was felt that it would be important to tell the story of several of these schools in which a global perspective had been or was being developed. The enthusiasm with which project directors responded when they were asked to contribute to this volume was gratifying.

The definition of global education which is used here is drawn from a number of sources, and it seems appropriate for all of the projects described in this volume:

> Global education involves learning about those problems and issues which cut across national boundaries, and about the interconnectedness of systems—cultural, ecological, economic, political, and technological...

> Global education also involves learning to understand and appreciate our neighbors with different cultural backgrounds from ours; to see the world through the eyes, and minds of others; and to realize that other people may view life differently than we do, and yet that all the people of the world need and want much the same things.[9]

Before beginning a discussion of what the reader can expect to find in subsequent chapters, the point must be made that global education, in addition to better preparing our children and youth for their future lives, also can serve to reinvigorate teachers and add new and exciting purpose to what has too often become a routine and uninteresting set of tasks in the classrooms of America. Time and time again, in project after project, teachers have been heard to say such things as "I'm excited about teaching again," "What we are doing here is so important," "I look forward to coming to school again." Such enthusiasm seems to spread to students, also.

In the next ten chapters, individual school projects from around the country are described. Most of these projects were begun in the mid- or late-eighties and most continue to-date. In each case, the author(s) tell about the setting at the beginning of the program: the community, the student body, the faculty, the school, and the curriculum. The global education project itself, and how it was initiated, is discussed. The various leadership roles played by key actors such as superintendents, principals, and lead teachers are noted, and linkages of the schools to global education knowledge are observed. Finally, problems which have arisen and prospects for the future of each project are examined, and significant learnings are identified.

In the final chapter, common themes which emerge from the various case studies are examined. This includes noting successful strategies which have been employed, as well as problems and roadblocks which seem to be persistent and which must be dealt with by those who would attempt to globalize the curriculum of a school.

This is not a "how-to-do-it" book. None of the authors mean to suggest that they have *the* answers to questions about how to globalize. The book has two purposes. First, through a description of practice in a variety of settings, there is an attempt to add to that body of knowledge generally thought of as educational change theory and, more specifically, there is a wish to assist with the beginning of a new body of knowledge having to do with creating a global perspective in schools.

Second, we do hope that, by telling the stories of a number of schools, people will be given some ideas about what they might do in their own settings. A set of schools with varied characteristics has been selected and it is assumed that the reader can identify with at least one of the schools described here. Perhaps more important, it is believed that the various themes—e.g., the role of leadership, how time is allocated, the role of linkage agents, district support, community attitudes—will have relevance for many interested readers.

In this set of cases, there are urban schools, rural schools and suburban schools. There are schools with predominantly minority student populations, ones with mixed ethnicity and ones with mainly white student bodies. High schools, middle schools and elementary schools are represented. Most every region of the country is included: the northeast, northwest, southwest, south, southeast, and midwest.

There are many fine programs around the country which are not described in this volume and as stated earlier, the number is growing. There are also many administrators, teachers, and lay persons who are interested in getting something started at their own schools. This book is dedicated to all of these people, the ones who are involved and the ones who wish to get involved. We hope that it is of value to them. Most important, we hope that the book adds to the dialogue about the question, *"What does it take to bring a global perspective to the curriculum of a school?"*

NOTES

1. John I. Goodlad, in James M. Becker (ed.), *Schooling for a Global Age*. New York: McGraw-Hill Book Co., 1979, p. xiii.

2. Kenneth A. Tye (ed.) *Global Education: From Thought to Action*. Alexandria, Va: Association for Supervision and Curriculum Development, 1990.

Barbara Benham Tye and Kenneth A. Tye, *Global Education: A Study of School Change*. Albany, New York: SUNY Press, forthcoming.

3. Chadwick F. Alger. *Your City in the World/The World in Your City: Discover the International Activities and Foreign Policies of People, Groups, and Organizations in Your Community*. Columbus, Ohio: Mershon Center, The Ohio State University, 1974.

4. Barney S. Glaser and Anselm Strauss. *The Discovery of Grounded Theory: Strategies for Qualitative Research*. Chicago: Aldine Publishing Co., 1967.

5. Herbert Blumer. *Symbolic Interaction: Perspective and Method*. Englewood Cliffs, NJ: Prentice-Hall, 1969.

6. Kenneth A. Tye, "Changing Our Schools: The Realities," *Study of Schooling Technical Report #30*. Los Angeles, Ca: Laboratory in School and Community Relations, UCLA, 1981.

7. Ernest L. Boyer. *High School: A Report on Secondary Education in America*. New York: Harper & Row, 1983. John I. Goodlad. *A Place Called School*. New York: McGraw Hill, 1984. Theodore R. Sizer, *Horace's Compromise: The Dilemma of the American High School*. Boston: Houghton Mifflin, 1984.

8. Ronald G. Havelock. *Planning for Innovation Through Dissemination and Utilization of Knowledge*. Ann Arbor, Mich: Institute for Social Research, University of Michigan, 1971. Also Nicholas Nash and Jack Culbertson (eds.) *Linking Processes in Educational Improvement*. Columbus, Ohio: University Council for Educational Administration, 1977.

9. Robert G. Hanvey. *An Attainable Global Perspective*. Denver, Colo: The Center for Teaching International Relations, 1976. Willard Kniep, "Defining a Global Education By Its Content," *Social Education*, October 1986, pp.437-446. Study Commission on Global Education, *The United States Prepares For Its Future: Global Perspectives in Education*. New York: Global Perspectives in Education, 1987.

CHAPTER TWO

TAOS HIGH SCHOOL

George Otero

Taos High School, in northeastern New Mexico, developed a strong international program by accident—the kind of accident that may be a more accurate description of how schools change than 90% of the literature we now read that presupposes a rational decision-making process in our schools. A group of teachers got together for a beer one Friday afternoon in 1986, and, a little more than a year later, an important program had evolved. As a result, this case may be instructive not as a model to be followed, but as a story with lessons to be gleaned.

IN THE BEGINNING

Beginnings are often elusive and hard to trace, especially in the schools where events often are non-linear and non-rational. But every story starts somewhere, and this one starts with an impromptu Friday afternoon get-together at the Mabel Dodge Luhan House, a well-known Taos landmark now used as an educational retreat center called Las Palomas de Taos. No one is sure today as to who gathered the group together, or why. Whatever the motivation for meeting, the teachers had a great time and decided to meet again and again and again.

The first five or six meetings had no particular focus, except for friendship and camaraderie. As the group met, ate together, and talked, eventually possibilities for change at their school began to surface in the discussions. Why not start a summer humanities program for high school students that would really involve them in the state's unique history and culture? How about starting a summer language camp, or perhaps an alternative school at a ranch in the mountains? Why not become the first rural international high school with a program that would relate vocational education as well as humanities and foreign language to global realities? Ideas were popping.

As thoughts were shared, the teachers discovered and learned to value each others' differences—and there were many. Three-fourths of the men and women in the group were Hispanic, but some were staunch Republicans while others were determined Democrats. Some belonged to the American Federation of Teachers; others to the National Education Association. There were teachers of math, science, history, agriculture, home economics, Russian, and English present, along with counselors and librarians.

The teachers in this group were also very much aware of what they considered to be the unique aspects of their community and the ways in which these influenced the high school. Taos is a town populated by people who carry a sense of history and culture with them day in and day out. Decisions are made with the weight of hundreds of years behind them. In Taos, you can't often get away with a viewpoint that ignores strongly-held perceptions of the past. You would get nowhere in Taos if you brought in a new educational program and tried to sell it on the basis that it worked in some other school or district. As they brainstormed, the teachers knew they would have to settle on an idea which would be unique, one which would address the needs of youth whom they considered to be different, and very special.

In other respects, however, Taos High school is not unlike other high schools across the nation. Its population of 800 typical 10-12th graders is 90% Hispanic and 10%

Native American. Dropout rates run at about the national average, 25-30% in this town of less than 25,000 residents. With the exception of the Russian course, taught by one unusual teacher, the curriculum is one that might be found at any small rural American high school.

After six months of meeting informally, chewing the fat and thinking big, the group—now numbering about ten— decided to take one idea and see if they could make it work. What was the impetus to action? The motives were, no doubt, complex and varied for each individual, but a major factor was a feeling that things could be better and that they, the teachers, might be able to initiate a change that they wanted. Teachers in general are a most hopeful group, though working in schools can teach them to be cautious. Too many teachers stop trusting their instincts, and enthusiasm and innovation are the first victims. These Taos High School teachers had created a way of working together that encouraged them to once again affirm their commitment by *creating*, and not simply managing, educational opportunities for young people.

The first idea that caught the group's fancy was not international education, but a summer program for students from around New Mexico to spend time in Taos studying the languages, culture, arts, and histories of the area.

The group needed a budget, a curriculum, and direction. The teachers divided up the tasks and went to work. Each successive meeting seemed to take longer than the last, as the work groups reported on their progress and each aspect of the project was thoroughly discussed. No one was willing to give up the fun or the food, either, so sessions from 6:00 to 11:00 pm became the norm.

Finally, after hours of thinking, writing, and discussion, the group concluded that their chances of beginning the next summer looked about as good as teachers getting a decent salary increase from the state legislature. Everyone was so busy with school activities that the summer institute placed too great a burden on time and energy. Their own research, thus, had led the teachers to seek a new direction—not an uncommon occurrence in a school improvement effort fueled primarily by the creative process.

Next, the group decided to consider an activity which would enrich their regular work at the high school, instead of planning for a summer institute. An international high school seemed to offer opportunities for everyone, regardless of subject taught.

At this point, the teachers sought the help of Las Palomas de Taos staff members who had experience in global education projects. Together, they agreed to do three things. First, the group wanted to reach consensus on a working definition of global/international education; one they all felt they could live with. This is easier said than done, because in any group invariably there will be a range of interpretations to be negotiated before shared meaning emerges. It was helpful to have a facilitator for this process.

Second, the group learned as much as they could about other global education projects around the United States and studied the writings of other educators to learn about the theoretical and conceptual underpinnings of global education. Finally, the facilitator helped the teachers compose a procedure they could use to explain their ideas to others.

As work on these three tasks began, meetings took on a more serious tone, reflecting the commitment of the ten educators to a common goal. They all wanted something special and different at Taos High School, in their classrooms, between themselves as professionals, and for the students. Pursuit of an international program was their vehicle. In a sense there was no stopping them, even though no one knew what lay ahead or what the program would look like in any detail. Vision and a sense of purpose are essential elements of any school reform; those who have to make the changes had best be the ones with the vision and the desire.

THE OBSTACLE COURSE

The idea "went public" at a Board of Education meeting in July of 1987, ten months after that first Friday afternoon get-together. The superintendent, who was supportive of the work that had been done thus far by the *ad hoc* teacher group, presented a funding proposal to the Board. It was short and sweet:

A CONCEPT FOR DEVELOPING AN INTERNATIONAL PROGRAM AT TAOS HIGH SCHOOL

For the past four years a number of programs and events have occurred for the benefit of students at the high school, with the goal of increasing their skill and understanding in the international arena.

For the past six months, a teacher group from the high school has been meeting to brainstorm ways to make international education available to more and more students at the high school.

THE GOAL

Have Taos High School be the first rural high school in the United States to have a comprehensive vocational-based international studies and foreign language program.

STEPS

Have the school board approve the goal.

Have a task force formed to address four tasks:

1. Plan implementation of experimental programs for the upcoming 87- 88 school year.

2. Design the structure of a program that would begin in earnest during the 88-89 school year.

3. Plan inservice activities to prepare professional staff to teach in the program.

4. Develop funding proposals and seek funds to run a substantial portion of the program for the first three years.

The board of education accepted the goal and approved Chapter 2 funds to the tune of $7,000 to assist the task force during the 1987-88 school year. The group, now officially known as the Taos High School International Studies Task Force, was well on its way. Where this was all headed specifically, no one could predict, but they were "off to see the wizard," and no one wanted to be left behind. Getting people to the once- or twice-a-month meetings was not a problem; attendance usually ran at about 90%. The task force clearly felt ownership of its project.

1987-88 was a year of muddling. The dough had been made, but it now had to rise and be formed into shape. The district had given them the tools to experiment, and they did. A September 1987 task force meeting was full of questions, such as "What is global education?" "What do we do with the professional time?" "How do we get students involved?" "What direction should we take?" and "Where are we at this point?"

If the task force had questions, they soon found out that the rest of the staff and administration at the high school had just as many, if not more. Some viewed the project as an idea that was being imposed on the whole school by just a handful of teachers; they wanted no part of it, whatever it was. The task force understood why other teachers were leery. New programs and curricula were introduced year after year. Like teachers everywhere, the Taos High staff had seen new initiatives come and go. They had little time or energy for another short-lived project.

Task force members knew that the legitimate concerns of their peers had to be addressed before any further planning was done. Clearly, this would have to be their first step. But it proved to be a difficult and trying task. Despite their attempt to be considerate and include everyone, the group frequently had to withstand verbal abuse, innuendo, intolerance and accusations from colleagues and administrators. Each and every crisis brought the task force together to listen to other views, to renew their own commitment and to decide together on positive and constructive responses to each problem as it occurred. They tried a variety of strategies: throughout the year, task force members presented ideas, offered to share materials and resources, and invited other faculty members to join the group for the special curriculum development inservices that were taking place at regular intervals.

The task force had several things working in its favor. First, it was broad-based; its ten members represented nearly every department of the high school. Second, it was composed of many of the strongest teachers in the school. No one could question their skill, professionalism, or dedication. Third, the group contained a number of the most powerful informal leaders on the Taos High faculty. These were not necessarily department chairs; but they were the people the other faculty had, in the past, listened to and respected.

Despite these advantages, by the end of the 87-88 year the task force had grown to just fifteen. Approximately thirty teachers on the faculty of 40-45 steadfastly refused to get involved. Many saw the project as just another way of depleting already-scarce funds, money which they felt should be used for other needs at the school. Others felt no ownership or interest in the project, partly because they hadn't been included from the beginning.

Then, too, it was clear to everyone that the principal didn't really support the project, either. At one point that year, he presented the entire faculty with a list of all of the various programs and projects in existence at the school and asked each person to rank them according to how important he or she felt each program or project was. When these data were tabulated, the international program ranked near the bottom, despite the high rankings given it by the teachers who were actually involved with it. The principal presented the results to the faculty at a later meeting, and the implication was that this program really lacked solid support at the school. This was quite a divisive tactic by the principal, and left the task force members feeling isolated. They concentrated their energies on developing the courses that were, they hoped, to become a permanent part of the school's curriculum.

By the spring of 1988, the task force had reluctant permission from the Taos High School administration to offer courses to all students for the upcoming year that would have an international focus. *If* students signed up for these course in sufficient numbers, classes would be held. The results were gratifying—with the exception of one math class, every course that was offered was filled. In fact, there had to be *three* sections of the new international foods class and two sections of the new environmental science class in order to meet the demand. A new course in international business was filled, as were the newly "internationalized" sections of honors English. Enrollment in foreign languages began to rise, also.

THE FIRST TWO YEARS

The focus of activity for the participating faculty during the 1988-89 year was to teach these new courses, using their experiences to develop a really solid curriculum containing an international emphasis. During that year, consultants from the Center for Teaching International Relations at the University of Denver provided inservice training for the teachers on the task force and any other interested teachers in the district. The goal was to develop learning activities and teaching units for each course that contained a global dimension.

The task force also won an important strategic victory that first year: the members wrote up their project and submitted it to the New Mexico Research and Study Council's annual competition for "best high school program of 1988-89"—*and won!* This external recognition of the program was what finally convinced the principal of its value. From then on, he became a supporter of the international high school concept. In fact, he agreed to release one teacher from teaching two periods a day to serve as half-time site coordinator for the project, beginning in September of 1989.

In the 1989-90 school year, the internationalized courses that had been pilot-tested the year before were offered again, and three new courses were added: math/computers/problem solving, Third World literature, and U.S. History with a global perspective. These proved to be just as popular as the others had been. One way or another, it seemed safe to say that every student at Taos High School was being touched by the new program.

By the middle of the 89-90 year, the program was rolling along pretty well. Although it still involved only about one-third of the faculty, that group had achieved something that is relatively rare in American education: they had developed and put into place an innovative curriculum, and they had made it work *using only the resources at hand*. Once the courses had been developed, pilot-tested, and revised, further external funding was not needed. And because teacher turnover is extremely rare at Taos High School, as long as the teachers on the task force remain on the faculty, the program is likely to continue.

Task force members continue to reach out to faculty members who have not yet participated in the program. The hostilities evident during the previous year were not present in 89-90. In fact, things have settled down and most people in the school, as well as in the Taos community, now view the international program as just another school activity, like band or sports or clubs; it has become a part of this particular school's culture.

LOOKING AHEAD

The international studies program at Taos High School was initiated by teachers and has been led by teachers through its first two years of implementation. In making their original idea work, these teachers had to learn to conceive of their jobs in new ways, making time for new ideas, courses, and activities. They did this, and are still doing it, because they believe that global awareness will broaden the horizons of their students and also because they have come to feel interest in, and ownership of, the change process itself.

But good teachers need more than their own desire and good intentions to change a school. They need support and encouragement in many forms, from everyone on all fronts. Task force members know that continued community support is essential for their program, and are forming an advisory group of community leaders who will serve both a support and a liaison function. Thus, going into the 1990-91 school year—the third year of the international curriculum—the program will have a new "stamp of approval" from the community. This should help to keep the momentum high as the program enters the third, and most critical, year.

Innovative programs often founder in the third or fourth year of implementation. Most often this is because, at this time, the original external funding is withdrawn and the program is expected to stand on its own feet. Because the Taos program never had major external funding, this shouldn't be a problem. Another reason change efforts sometimes lose momentum in the third or fourth year has to do with teacher turnover: the faculty members who felt original ownership move on to other schools, or retire, and newly-hired teachers are inadequately initiated into the project. Again, this should not be much of a problem at Taos, where teacher turnover is traditionally low.

What weakens the Taos program is the polarization of the faculty into participants and non-participants. This, too, is a common problem with educational innovation and sometimes it can create enough divisiveness within a faculty to bring a program down. As this book goes to press, it doesn't look as if this will happen at Taos High School because the participating teachers are popular and well respected, both in the school and in the community. Drawing the non-participants into the program remains the primary challenge facing the task group; when this has been accomplished, Taos High can *really* call itself an International High School.

CHAPTER THREE

DECATUR HIGH SCHOOL

Gary Howard

Kathy Purcell, principal of Decatur High School near Seattle, Washington, wanted to reach the "kids in the middle." She was concerned that they were not served by either honors or special education programs, and were not as well educated as they could be.

So when she learned of the program to put global studies into the school, spearheaded by a local global education center, she knew it was right for her school. "I was looking for a teacher-directed vehicle to overcome an entrenched and tradition-bound curriculum," she said.

The Decatur High School Global Studies Program grew out of a regional program that had been ongoing since the 1982-83 school year. At that time, a small group of educators came together to discuss a new effort in high school multicultural and global education. The result of their planning was the creation of the Global REACH (Respecting Ethnic and Cultural Heritage) Consortium, or GRC. The goal of GRC was to create interdisciplinary teams of teachers working together at the school site level to design global education strategies.

In the spring of 1983, they unveiled their plans to a group of administrators, including the Assistant Superintendent of the Federal Way School District, Ted Gartner. He in turn brought the ideas back to the district's high school administrators, including Purcell, and invited their participation.

THE COMMUNITY AND THE SCHOOL

Purcell's Decatur High School is in Federal Way, Washington, on the Puget Sound midway between the busy ports of Seattle and Tacoma. The town population, nearing the 100,000 mark, is 94 percent white, with the remainder a scattering of Asians, blacks, and Native Americans.

Federal Way is a young, white-collar, and affluent community. Fifty-four percent of the residents are between 25 and 44 years of age, and 66 percent of the employed adults have annual incomes greater than $25,000. More than half of the adults have attended college, with 20 percent having finished at least four years. Thirty-six percent of all jobs in the city are in professional or managerial positions. One of the city's largest employers is the Weyerhauser Company, which has its world headquarters in Federal Way.

Decatur High School has its historical roots in an open-enrollment alternative program begun by the Federal Way School District in the early 1970's. Originally housed in portables, the program moved to a new open-concept facility in 1978. Beginning with large open spaces under one expansive roof, the school facilities and philosophy gradually evolved toward a more traditional classroom-centered focus. Portable walls were brought in to divide the spaces into separate classrooms, and finally in 1985 a major remodeling project transformed Decatur High into a traditional building with locker-lined hallways and solid-wall divisions between classrooms.

With 1,200 students in grades 10-12, Decatur High's economic and ethnic mix reflects the community. Thus, the students come somewhat disproportionately from middle and upper-middle income families, although there is a significant population of low-income students (5%

participate in the free lunch program, with perhaps twice that many eligible).

Decatur's faculty is an experienced group; most of the teachers have been in the classroom from 18 to 25 years. The faculty prides itself on being student-centered; most are active in extracurricular activities. The teaching staff of 54 is gender-balanced, as is the administrative staff. Almost ten percent of the teachers are minority. The principal characterizes the staff as "strong instructors" who place a high value on providing their students with a quality educational experience. Teaching, for the most part, tends to be departmentalized, and there is little collaboration across the various disciplines.

With the exception of the Global Studies Program described in this chapter, Decatur offers a standard comprehensive high school curriculum. Students are tracked into basic skills, regular, honors, and AP tracks, but students have the option of taking classes in any track. Sixty percent of Decatur graduates go on to college, with 30 percent attending four-year schools. Decatur offers one of the largest marketing programs in the state of Washington, with many students involved in business-related courses. A Japanese language program has been growing in popularity the past few years, and the school has a long history of foreign student exchange programs.

GETTING STARTED

When Kathy Purcell heard about the Consortium, she chose Carl Buchholz, a veteran teacher of 12th grade Contemporary World Problems, to head Decatur High's global studies team. "I chose Carl because he is respected as a scholar and a leader," said Purcell. "He has shown a commitment to quality teaching, and has a well-grounded global and international understanding."

Buchholz said he felt the need for his students to grow in their understanding of global issues beyond what he could provide in his classroom. He saw the GRC as an opportunity to expand and strengthen what he was already doing. Buchholz and Purcell set about recruiting teachers to join them. "We wanted teachers who were leaders in their departments and were willing to try something new," said Buchholz. "We were looking for teachers who were committed to quality teaching, who didn't bind themselves to a textbook, who were demanding of students, and who shared our concern that students become effective global citizens."

The two educators attracted a core group of teachers to join them, and formed the Decatur High School global studies team. The members, who represented the fields of social studies, language arts, science, art, and foreign languages, cited a variety of personal and professional reasons for joining the team. "Little was being done to teach students about their world today," said Keith Forrest. As a veteran world history teacher, Forrest said he felt weighed down by a textbook he could never finish. Without an opportunity to study post-World War II issues, his students had little sense of how their lives related to history.

Bonnie Peterson said she always wanted to teach global environmental issues in her science classes, but didn't know how to fit them into the curriculum. She saw her involvement with global studies as an opportunity to teach new content.

Art teacher Russ Hamamoto saw team membership as consistent with his personal style of teaching. "I am never truly satisfied with the 'sameness' in things," he said. "I'm willing to venture out and try new ideas and programs, and I'm continually changing and evolving." Hamamoto added that he wanted to help students move beyond their biases and prejudices, and move away from the notion that "the U.S.A. is the center of the universe."

Foreign language teacher Linda Reed believed global education could provide "an institutionalized approach to my personal goal of making my students better world citizens."

"Teaching sophomore English had fallen into a near-deadly cycle," said 20-year veteran Pat Smith. "The chance to let fresh air into the curriculum was irresistible." Smith added that she was motivated by the desire to renew her own excitement about teaching, despite the fact that it meant "launching out into lonely, untraveled regions of study."

The teachers wanted to improve the learning experience for their students, and they wanted to renew and enliven teaching for themselves. They were committed, quality educators who were willing to invest time, energy and enterprise in a journey that had no definite destination. What resulted from their efforts, and what they learned in the process, was well worth their investment.

FIRST STEPS TOGETHER

In the fall of 1983, the Decatur H.S. team attended the first symposium sponsored by the Global REACH Consortium, "The State of the Earth and the State of the Art in Global Education." The session brought together interdisciplinary teams of high school teachers from eight Puget Sound area school districts. There, the Decatur team was challenged to think about the goals of global education and begin planning a common project for their school.

Three months later, the consortium brought everyone together again in a two-day retreat setting where they heard major addresses on global issues and attended sessions on classroom applications. The teams were then given several hours to design specific plans for their own schools and districts. It was during this process that the Decatur team came up with the idea of creating a "global perspectives track"—a sequence of courses which any student could opt to follow through his or her three years at Decatur High. The team wanted to internationalize the curriculum by introducing more global perspectives, concepts, and content into selected required courses and electives. Students would then have the option of meeting several of their graduation and college entrance requirements within the program. "We were like a nuclear reactor, feeding on each other's ideas," one teacher observed. "It was exciting, refreshing, and renewing to work with the global studies team; the commitment and creativity was inspiring."

During the months following the retreat, the team worked out the details of their plan and won school board approval to launch the pilot Global Studies Program. Beginning with the 1985-86 school year, they redesigned sections of two required sophomore courses, World History and World Literature. Entering sophomores were given the choice of taking these courses taught in the regular format, or infused with a global perspective. Global World History, which replaced the Western Civilization course, emphasized the Third World, the Pacific Rim, and the Soviet Union. The global World Literature course included authors from Asia, Latin America and Africa as well as from Europe and the West.

During that school year, the team worked to plan the junior level courses to be offered the following year: Global Ecology and Asian Art. In similar fashion, the senior Global Studies Seminar was designed while the first round of junior year courses was being taught. Thus, at the end of three years, a strand of global studies courses had been developed to allow students to "major" in international studies (Course descriptions are included at the end of the chapter).

THE PROGRAM IN PLACE

The 1987-88 school year was the first year that classes were functioning at all three grade levels. The chart below provides an overview of enrollment in the courses during the three-year development phase:

GLOBAL STUDIES PROGRAM ENROLLMENT				
(One section represents approximately 30 students)				

Course	Grade	85-86	86-87	87-88
World History	10	2 sections	6 sections	6 sections
World Literature	10	2 sections	4 sections	5 sections
Global Ecology	11		1 section	2 sections
Asian Art	11		1 section	1 section
Global Studies Seminar	12			1 section
Approximate number of students:		120	360	450

Throughout their three years at Decatur, students in the Global Studies Program are encouraged to study at least one foreign language. Being bilingual is seen as an integral part of achieving a global perspective. During the years since full implementation of the program, enrollment and interest in foreign languages have increased steadily, particularly in Spanish and Japanese.

Student interest in global issues also led to the founding of a Human Rights Club. More than 120 students have joined, and many of the club's leaders have come from the global education program.

One of the most exciting features of the Decatur program is the degree to which teachers from different disciplines have cooperated in developing course offerings. World History and World Literature are coordinated at several levels to allow students to simultaneously study the literary achievements and the historical and political content related to a specific nation or region. With the program functioning at all three grade levels, students can see consistency and continuity in the curriculum and gain a sense that their knowledge of the world is being deepened and broadened over time.

Another strength of the program is that it has provided teachers with a sense of camaraderie they had not known before. They gather together several times a year for dinner parties, and manage to integrate fun along with the work they do. One of the team members described her early efforts to develop new courses as akin to "flying without a net." She feels that the personal and professional support of the team was necessary in giving her the strength to abandon her old, familiar program and begin teaching from a global perspective—without being constrained by textbooks.

LEADERSHIP AND LINKAGES

The Assistant Superintendent of the Federal Way School District made the initial contact with the Global REACH Consortium, and was the key central office person responsible for designating and releasing funds to support team activities. The Decatur High School principal accepted the invitation to become involved in Consortium membership. She and the Assistant Superintendent shared a strong commitment to multicultural and equity education, and knew that global/international understanding was a critical area in need of attention at the high school level. In addition, the principal had been engaged in a process of educational reform at Decatur and felt that the global education team might provide an effective vehicle for instructional improvement. She selected Carl Buchholz as the team leader, and then allowed him a great deal of freedom in recruiting the rest of the team.

Carl's style in leading the Global Studies team has been collegial and collaborative. He provides the link between the team, the principal, the district office, and the Consortium. He encourages a mutually supportive and respectful atmosphere among team members, and they in turn demonstrate a great deal of acceptance and appreciation of his leadership. Through Carl, the team has also established a valuable link to the district's curriculum director. They have benefited greatly from her assistance and expertise in the process of developing new global perspectives units and courses for their program. This link has also helped forge a bond between the Global Studies Program and the regular, ongoing curriculum development strategies of the district.

Leadership of the Decatur Global Studies Program has been a team effort. Each of the teachers involved is an instructional leader within his or her own department. Team members were selected on the basis of their commitment to quality teaching and their openness to new instructional approaches. Each member of the team has taken on the task of redesigning his or her curriculum to provide a more global, multicultural, and international focus. They have shared their materials and their expertise with other teachers in their fields, both at Decatur and within the network of the Consortium.

THE GLOBAL REACH CONSORTIUM

The development of the Decatur Global Studies Program has been supported throughout its history by the structure and process of the Global REACH Consortium. The GRC is a collaborative membership organization in the Puget Sound region involving educators from local school districts, institutions of higher education, the state department of education, and community groups concerned with international issues. (The Global REACH Consortium is described at the end of the Chapter)

Several area universities have provided a rich source of materials for the GRC. The consortium has utilized people from the University of Washington, Pacific Lutheran University and Western Washington University to clarify teachers' understanding of a variety of topics. From defining issues in central America and placing the Middle East conflict into an historical context, to providing an introduction to the rich literature of the Third World and to elucidating lay people's understanding of the complex global economic system, a wide variety of topics have been covered with the help of university scholars.

Another key link to the universities has been the presence on the GRC Steering Committee of the directors of the various outreach centers at the University of Washington's Henry M. Jackson School of International Studies. These individuals provide direct access to a rich array of resources related to East Asia, South Asia, the Middle East and the Soviet Union. They, along with staff members in the University Extension Program, have consistently contributed to the planning and implementation of GRC inservice programs. Contacts at the universities have also made it possible to offer university credit options for GRC teachers who wish to expand their knowledge in specific areas.

Besides drawing on the universities, the consortium is committed to bringing teachers into direct contact with significant players on the multicultural and global stages. For a symposium on Mexico, a prominent opposition leader within the dominant PRI political party was brought to Seattle to address the GRC membership. For a conference on the global economic system, a leading female economist from Pakistan provided a Third World feminist perspective. For a conference on environmental issues, a Native American healer/poet/psychotherapist was asked to provide an indigenous person's perspective on the earth as a holistic system. Such exposure to primary source information and individuals is an invaluable experience for consortium members.

The GRC has also brought the Decatur team into contact with a broad base of global education expertise outside the Puget Sound region. The GRC leadership has actively engaged in building a national network of organizations which provide international education at the K-12 level. Through participation in this national network, the consortium has significantly broadened the exposure of its members to materials, knowledge, and approaches to global education. The leaders of many of these major centers and programs have come to observe and provide expertise for various GRC activities. In this way, the Decatur team has not had to work out its unique program in isolation from other global educators, but has benefited from direct and ongoing contact with some of the best thinking in the field.

PROBLEMS AND PROBLEM-SOLVING

The Decatur team did encounter a number of problems. For example, several teachers reported frustration in searching for curriculum materials relating to global or international content. "The publishing world is simply not ready for this revolution in education," said English teacher Pat Smith. The Decatur team had to develop their own curriculum resources. To address this need, they contacted their district curriculum director and requested an inservice dealing with specific models and skills to help them in course development.

Early in the process of development, the team became aware that some parents and students might perceive the program as an exclusive offering for only the brightest scholars. Global studies could acquire a mystique of elitism that could cause some students to avoid the classes. To combat this, team members began going to the district junior high schools to explain the program to ninth graders prior to their selection of sophomore year classes. This proved to be a highly effective technique for recruiting a healthy cross-section of students. However, an administrative decision at the district level forced the team to discontinue its orientation activities.

The success of the program during the second and third years created another problem: how to recruit more teachers to cover the increased class load of students wanting to participate. The team soon discovered that not all teachers were willing to "...fly without a net." They were presented with the new challenge of packaging their materials, units, and courses for teachers who were not as informed about global education.

The Decatur team is also concerned about the issue of continued funding for their program. As long as they are perceived as a "special program," they are vulnerable to the whims of shifting district priorities and administrative personnel changes. They feel fortunate that the Federal Way School District has supported them during the developmental period. However, it is clear that they must become a regular part of the ongoing program if their efforts are to continue. For this reason, the team has initiated— along with the district curriculum director—a process of formal evaluation of the program. With a favorable outcome, they hope to establish the Global Studies Program as a part of the regular curriculum.

With her commitment to equity and multicultural education, the Decatur principal has expressed some concern that the increased emphasis on global issues and international content may detract from the attention given to dealing with cultural diversity in the United States. A strength of the Decatur team is its awareness of this issue, and the work the team has done to provide for the necessary linking of multicultural and global education.

Decatur team members want to share their Global Studies Program with other Federal Way District high schools, but have encountered resistance. In the minds of several observers, the primary obstacle seems to be professional jealousy. Apparently, the program is perceived by other teachers as being the "property" of the Decatur team. Other teachers resist the notion of using "someone else's program." There is an apparent sense that by adopting the Global Studies Program at the other schools in the district, those teachers would be acknowledging the superiority of this approach over their present program. It is difficult to see how this barrier might be overcome.

LOOKING AHEAD

At this point, the Global Studies Program is well established at Decatur High School. The team now wants to refine the program, package it effectively and offer it to a broader audience. The future employers of the students will benefit directly from the Global Studies Program, so it is hoped that the corporate sector may, therefore, be interested in helping to fund the team's efforts. So the future holds the exciting promise of moving outside the walls of public education to form partnerships with private enterprise as co-sponsors of high-quality global perspectives education.

CONCLUDING THOUGHTS

After several years of this project, there have been a number of significant learnings. Major among them are:

1. Time and Change. The Decatur team has demonstrated that positive school change takes time and ongoing commitment. The change process itself seems to follow a three-stage sequence, beginning with **Awareness**, moving on to **Implementation**, and finally to issues of **Institutionalization**. During the Awareness stage, the Decatur team members worked on questions of defining global education and exploring their own understanding of how it might relate to their various disciplines. When they entered the Implementation stage, they were concerned with identifying resources, trying out new teaching strategies in their classrooms, and eventually developing new courses. They are now in the Institutionalization stage, dealing with issues of packaging their units and courses for efficient use by other teachers, and moving their program into acceptance as a regular and ongoing part of their school's curriculum.

2. Professional Support. The Decatur team was given the opportunity, through Consortium membership, to participate in an ongoing process of professional development related to global education. They were not merely handed their curriculum development task and told to "go forth and be creative," as happens too often in educational change efforts. Rather, team members were given release time on a regular basis to attend Consortium conferences, meet together as a team, and redesign their courses.

One of the team members noted, "I was given the resources and materials and time to write a course that I felt was needed at the high school level." Providing teachers with this kind of professional support was an essential element in creating effective school change at Decatur High.

3. Teacher Professionalism and Renewal. Participants in the GRC activities generally agree that teachers too often work in isolation, and have very little opportunity to share with other professionals. According to principal Purcell, "Teachers have not had much chance to 'retreat,' to interact intellectually and professionally together outside the classroom." She said the consortium has provided "the best model available" for teacher professionalism and renewal. By giving teachers ongoing opportunities for creative time together and providing students with a global education, the Decatur High School Global Studies Program has helped reinvigorate quality teachers and helped to prepare global leaders for the 21st century.

*   *   *   *   *   *   *   *   *   *

DECATUR HIGH'S GLOBAL STUDIES PROGRAM: COURSES

SOPHOMORE YEAR

World History Global Studies: This course replaces the traditional Western Civilization approach to world history. Greater emphasis is given to Third World, Pacific Rim, and Soviet realities. Instead of getting lost in the past, the curriculum emphasizes the period from 1930 to the present. Rather than relying on a textbook, up-to-date student readings are gathered by the teacher from a variety of sources. Mini-unit topics include hunger, nuclear power, world agencies, human rights, trade, and the environment.

Global Studies in Literature: This course moves beyond the normal European and Western offerings of most world literature classes. Cross-cultural concepts from the field of anthropology are introduced, the culturally diverse roots of the English language are explored, and issues involved in the English-as-the-official-language debate are illuminated. Students are engaged in reading representative authors from Korea, China, Central and South Africa, the Soviet Union, Japan, India, Latin America, and Europe.

JUNIOR YEAR

Global Ecology: This course provides an option for meeting one of the Science requirements for graduation and college entrance. It provides students with a well-rounded background of knowledge related to contemporary global environmental issues, including deforestation, resource depletion, pollution, animal extinction and the interdependence of ecosystems. Emphasis is given to helping students gain the skills to make informed personal, societal, and career decisions about environmental issues that affect their lives.

Asian Art: This class provides students with an introduction to the rich an ancient artistic heritage of several countries, including China, Japan, India, Indonesia, Korea, and Southeast Asia. The course also explores contemporary Asian art and the extensive influence many forms of Asian art have exerted on the West.

SENIOR YEAR

Global Studies Senior Seminar: This course may be chosen by students to meet the traditional Contemporary World Problems requirement. Emphasis is given to independent research projects and to seminar-style interaction of students. Students are actively involved in a problem-solving approach to global issues and the teacher continually challenges them to practice higher-level thinking skills.

Independent Global Studies: This one-semester elective allows students to independently explore in depth a global issue of interest to them. After winning approval of their research topic, students are encouraged to work with a variety of teachers to achieve an interdisciplinary perspective in their final project.

STRUCTURE OF THE GLOBAL REACH CONSORTIUM

The structure of the Global REACH Consortium is designed to provide an overall umbrella of support for activities which are locally determined by individual districts and building-level teams, and to make effective staff development programs and classroom materials more accessible to local educators. The key elements of the Consortium structure are the following:

1. *School District Commitment.* At the beginning of the school year, the superintendent of each member district signs a contract agreeing to the following conditions:

a. Payment of $1,000 for district membership in the Consortium, and an additional $500 for each team involved.

b. Formation of at least one building team consisting of one administrator and 4-8 teachers from diverse disciplines.

c. Designation of one district employee to serve on the Consortium Steering Committee.

d. Allocation of funds for at least five days of release time for each members of the building level team (some districts have more than one team).

e. Provision of adequate time and a process for each team to share its work with other teachers and buildings within the district.

2. *Building-level teams.* Interdisciplinary teams of teachers and administrators from participating school districts are the basic unit of organization and activity for the Consortium.

3. *Steering Committee.* A group of representatives from each of the participating districts and organizations meets regularly to oversee and direct the cooperative planning and decision-making of the Consortium.

4. *Advisory Council.* The Advisory Council is structured to provide a broad base of community support for the activities of the Consortium. Made up of key community leaders from diverse organizations and businesses, this group expands the fund raising capabilities of the Global REACH Consortium, as well as enhancing the experiential and knowledge base for generating effective curriculum and inservice programs.

5. *Staff.* Consortium activities are coordinated by a Program Director, who is on the staff of the REACH Center for Multicultural and Global Education, a non-profit educational organization providing training and materials to school districts throughout the country. The REACH Center staff, including the Executive Director, Assistant Director, other Program Directors, and clerical staff, all provide services to the Consortium at specific times throughout the year.

6. *Resource Library.* The Consortium is involved in an ongoing process of evaluating, acquiring, and disseminating to teachers high quality global/multicultural classroom materials and resources. In addition to materials for use in social studies classses, particular attention is given to identifying materials which apply global/multicultural concepts in disciplines other than social studies. The Consortium also has an interest in developing new teaching

units and classroom activities which are not presently available.

7. *Program.* Consortium teams are brought together for five days of inservice during the school year: a two-day symposium in the fall, a two-and-a-half day residential retreat and work session in the winter, and a one-day Share Fair in the spring. In addition, the building teams carry out programs and events in their own schools and districts throughout the year. Consortium staff members provide on-site workshops and follow-up at the request of the teams.

CHAPTER FOUR

JOSHUA EATON ELEMENTARY SCHOOL

Paul Mulloy

Today's children, the future citizens of the 21st century, will have to face complex issues such as environmental protection, energy use, food production and arms control. If students of the 1990s learn to think with a global perspective, they will be better equipped to cope with tomorrow's dilemmas.

That's the philosophy at the Joshua Eaton Elementary school, one of four elementary schools serving the residential community of Reading, Massachusetts, 15 miles northwest of Boston. With a middle- to upper-class population of 23,000, Reading tends to be moderately liberal, politically and socially.

The school system has a reputation for academic excellence in a region where expectations and parental involvement are high, and money, despite reduced tax revenues and declining enrollments, is available. In 1987, nearly 80 percent of the graduating high school class went on to college.

Nonetheless, this district, like most others in the commonwealth, has been hurt by the tax reform legislation of the early 80s. Teacher layoffs, contract disputes, and mounting frustration among an experienced faculty resulted in morale problems and skepticism regarding proposed innovations.

GETTING STARTED WITH GLOBAL EDUCATION

In 1985, Joshua Eaton faculty members launched an ambitious attempt to reform their school's curriculum using a global perspective. The initial efforts, led by library/media specialist Barbara McLean and fifth grade teacher Jean Weatherbee, were prompted by national assessment studies indicating that children are most open to learning about other peoples and cultures between the ages of seven and twelve—before the onset of puberty, when ethnocentrism and stereotypical thinking tend to set in.

With support from principal Donald Farnham and Reading Schools Assistant Superintendent Robert Munelly, McLean and Weatherbee made global education their underlying theme—providing better training for life in an age of global interdependence. Their goal was to infuse this ideal into as many courses and grade levels as possible.

Gaining the support of other faculty members, however, is often a difficult task. McLean and Weatherbee emphasized to their colleagues that learning and thinking with a global perspective did not mean stuffing a new course into the already overcrowded curriculum. In fact, it meant what Harlan Cleveland, of the Hubert H. Humphrey Institute for Public Affairs recently pointed out: "Every subject taught—science, history, geography, math, music, art and, most emphatically, the basics of reading and writing—provides an opportunity for introducing young people to global issues and concepts that help them understand that the world is round, fragile, and fully packed."(1)

THE CHINA CONNECTION

To begin their program to "globalize" instruction, in July 1985, Weatherbee, McLean, and two other Joshua Eaton teachers attended an institute at the Peabody Museum in Salem, Mass. The museum's collection concentrated on paintings from the China trade activities of New England ship captains. The program included three days devoted to lectures and historical and architectural talks. Two other days were spent developing curriculum materials and teaching strategies using the resources of the Peabody Museum. Participating teachers were encouraged to utilize the museum library and to use primary source documents including manuscripts, logs, and journals kept on the 19th century ships.

As a follow-up to the program, the Joshua Eaton team further refined an interdisciplinary maritime studies unit for fifth grade students. The unit was based on 19th century New England maritime activities and on the Hawaiian, Japanese and Chinese cultures the sailors encountered. China was selected by the team for special emphasis throughout the 1985-86 school year. On two field trips to the Peabody Museum, instruction was given on Chinese daily life and economic activities. Each session also included a drawing lesson for students. These sketches became the basis for more elaborate artworks and writing under the direction of Joshua Eaton art, media, and other classroom teachers.

As an extension of this program, McLean, along with art teacher William Nicklasson and school district art director Susan Wheitle, was named to the newly-formed Governor's Advisory Council on Guangdong Province, People's Republic of China. The council was the result of a five-year effort which began with the visit of a 19-member Massachusetts delegation to Guangdong to investigate ways to strengthen developing business ties between Massachusetts and China.

Since its inception, the Council has initiated trade, education and arts exchanges. The Joshua Eaton School was one of two elementary schools in the state represented on the Council. Nicklasson and Wheitle secured exchanges of art work and correspondence with Guangdong's Pei Zheng Elementary School. The first art work was sent east in November 1985, and a return packet was received from China shortly thereafter. In addition, in conjunction with the

Peabody Museum, an exchange of art was arranged with the Museum of History in Taipei, Taiwan.

WITH A LITTLE HELP FROM THEIR FRIENDS

To maintain Joshua Eaton's momentum, in January, 1986, the Massachusetts Global Education Program (MGEP), with help from the Harvard Graduate School of Education's Principals' Center, provided funding from the Danforth Foundation.

Since 1979, the Massachusetts Global Education Program, and its predecessor the Tri-States Global Studies Project, has assisted classroom teachers to become more proficient in the teaching of global, social science, and educational skills topics. More than 2,500 teachers, school administrators, and curriculum specialists have been given the opportunity to experience MGEP's programs and activities.

In 1982, the Program developed and published *Massachusetts and the World*, an activity and resource book designed to increase student awareness of the connections the world has with Massachusetts. From 1984 through 1987, the Program received funding from the Danforth Foundation to conduct summer institutes in global studies for teachers and administrators throughout New England. A continuing grant from the Danforth Foundation provided for teacher development workshops, minigrants to teachers to develop curriculum for their schools, and a special program for principals undertaken in collaboration with the Principals' Center at the Harvard Graduate School of Education.

The MGEP Resource Center houses a growing collection of A.V. materials, texts, simulations, computer software, lesson plans, and units which are available for use by teachers in eastern Massachusetts. The library includes reference books on many nations and cultures, background on contemporary issues and professional reading in global and geographic education.

In 1988, MGEP joined with the global education programs at Wellesley College and the Massachusetts Geographic Alliance at Salem State College, to present a three-week institute for selected Massachusetts teachers. The global education programs at Wellesley College were funded to promote international education among regional school districts. The Massachusetts Geographic Alliance is part of the National Geographic Society national network formed to stimulate the improvement of geography education in the curriculum.

The Danforth grant helped the Chinese culture come alive for Joshua Eaton students. A trip to Boston's Chinatown enabled them to visit a grocery store, sample candy, and meet with the residents. Further exchanges of students' art work, letters, and photographs were made with the Pei Zheng School. The district physical education staff and classroom teachers taught Chinese dances and exercises.

The teaching of global education, especially relating to China, was firmly established during the 1985-86 school year. The following summer, McLean, Weatherbee and 30 other educators attended "World Regions—The Local Connection," an MGEP-sponsored two-week institute. Through a variety of learning activities, the institute staff demonstrated how local and regional resources can be used to teach global issues in the classroom and how geographic, historical, and cultural connections can be made between the local community and other regions of the world.

JOSHUA EATON AND THE WORLD

As a result of their participation in the program, McLean and Weatherbee received a follow-up $500 Danforth mini-grant from MGEP to continue their program and to present workshops for their school staff. In addition, a session at the MGEP institute on grantsmanship helped McLean obtain a Massachusetts State Department of Education inservice grant of $2,000.

By combining this funding with financial support from the school's parent-teacher organization and the Massachusetts Chapter 188 School Improvement Act, the two teachers integrated all special programs for the 1986-87 school year under the title, "Joshua Eaton and the World."

To ensure that this theme would be understood and implemented by the rest of the staff, four consultants were hired to present workshops on various global studies topics. The consultants not only made in-service presentations to the teachers, but also worked directly with students in the classroom. The director of MGEP worked with a third grade class on a family origins activity; an early childhood education specialist demonstrated how games and toys from around the world can aid global understanding; the Senior China Specialist at Boston's Children's Museum worked with second, third, and fifth grade classes on Chinese language and writing; and the co-director of the Massachusetts Geography Alliance helped teachers and students understand how choices of settlement location are often based on geographic considerations. Assistant Superintendent Munelly even pitched in by teaching a fifth grade class on the geography of China.

Additional "Joshua Eaton and the World" events included "The Art of the Book," in which a resident artist helped children explore what books mean to us today and what role books play in other cultures. There was also folk art, informational fairs, puppet shows, storytellers, Chinese mythological animals painted on windows, and map projects ranging from the school floor plan to Joshua Eaton's connections with the world.

The 1986-87 school year culminated with a day-long China celebration open to parents, other teachers, and the general public. The students began that school day as Chinese youngsters do, with a drill of calisthenics. American students were further introduced to China through the eyes of specialists in martial arts, clothing, food, music, painting, and folk arts. Student art work was displayed, and a Chinese lunch was served.

THE WORD SPREADS

With the beginning of the 1987-88 school year, Assistant Superintendent Munelly was appointed superintendent, ensuring the Joshua Eaton staff that support for global education would continue.

McLean and Weatherbee began to present workshops to other district teachers. As the program became known outside of the Reading system, they were invited to share the "Joshua Eaton model" at a K-9 school seminar sponsored by Tufts University, and a Teachers Sharing Conference organized by the Masschusetts State Department of Education. They also became more active with the Governor's Advisory Council on Guangdong, and were frequently asked to meet with visiting Chinese school delegations to explain the Joshua Eaton curriculum.

The original curriculum was then broadened to include a focus on the Soviet Union. Using the same interdisciplinary approach that was used on China, and with the full support of the Joshua Eaton staff, information about the Soviet Union began to "explode" all over the school.

Map skills in the media center for all grades encompassed a variety of Soviet geographical data. Books of Russian folk tales were made available from the town library and from Educators for Social Responsibility (ESR), a national group (with a Cambridge chapter) specializing in peace and disarmament issues, including dispelling stereotypes about the USSR. Music specialist Sally Merchant targeted grades two through five with Russian songs, including music from the "Firebird" and the "1812 Overture."

First grade teacher Mary Leary invited her nephew to show slides and discuss his recent visit to the USSR, while Dr. Christine Redford's fifth graders were visited by parent

Joan McKinnon, a former Russian language instructor, who read the students some Russian poetry in Russian and English. Fifth grade teacher Ilene Grinker, who had also traveled in the Soviet Union, immersed her class in landmarks, tapes, video, music, dance, food, art, and fairy tales. Art director Wheltle and parent Ann Mark borrowed an exhibit of Soviet children's art from ESR, and traveled throughout the school district generating excitement and helping students understand that Soviets and Americans have similarities as well as cultural differences.

Capitalizing on their successful experience with China Day, the staff completed the school year by organizing a "Parade of Nations" information fair. Assisted by parent volunteers Rachel Baumgartner and Cathy Symonds, they arranged for guest speakers and collected materials for display. The day began with a parade around the school yard, the children choosing the country they wished to march with by lining up behind that country's flag. Presentations were made during the day by guests who had visited, lived in, or originally had come from other countries.

Along with the numerous projects they displayed, the presenters loaded their audiences with additional facts: in France, Sunday night dinner at grandmother's is still a tradition, soccer is the number one and just about only sport, and short pants are the rage for boys under twelve. Also, Scots bagpipers know as many as 800 songs by heart. India introduced most of the spices used by Americans today, and no matter where you stand in the Taj Mahal, you can see all six columns.

The students tasted such Russian treats as honey cakes, noodle pudding, tea with jam and borscht; from Greece, lamb, feta cheese, sausage, olives and honey were tried; and chile peppers, corn dough, hot chocolate with milk, cinnamon and sugar were sampled from Mexico. They participated in a Greek dance, a mock wedding ceremony, touched worry beads, and examined an 80-year-old hand-made tablecloth. They tried on hats and played with wooden toys, musical instruments and straw dolls from Mexico.

University graduate student Fatema Dahodwala asked the children if they knew what India's national pastime is. "Meditating?" asked one student. "It's movie making," Dahodwala responded. "India has the second largest population in the world. It makes more movies in one year than all of Hollywood. Indian actors sometimes make 35 films at the same time—and people can attend movies for about 50 cents."

As the end of the 1987-88 school year approached, McLean and Weatherbee's effectiveness in integrating global studies was evident in the participation of Reading School District teachers at all levels in MGEP Summer 1988 programs. Attending MGEP's summer institute and receiving follow-up Danforth mini-grants for the 1988-89 school year were Joshua Eaton art teacher Nicklasson, who was developing a display of children's art from around the world; Coolidge Middle School teachers Ellen Swenson and William McQuillan, who were organizing a geography center in their school library, and Reading High School history teacher Robert Swanson, who was developing a unit on post-WW II Soviet-American relations.

In addition, teachers from several Reading elementary schools participated in the second K-9 Seminar in Global Awareness, co-sponsored by MGEP and Tufts University. Along with McLean, Weatherbee, Nicklasson and Wheltle, several teachers also were named to a system-wide social studies curriculum committee, with the task of reporting to superintendent Munelly on how all subject matter disciplines at all grade levels may be infused with global studies themes. This should ensure that the changes which have taken place so far will be institutionalized into the Reading Schools curriculum in the future.

LESSONS LEARNED

The 1980's have been an exciting time for school reform. Recent studies such as the Carnegie report and the influence of Theodore Sizer's Effective Schools movement suggest that school leadership should be restructured to involve teachers more in a school's instructional leadership.

The staff at Joshua Eaton provided a good example of how this can work. They had a clear vision of what they wanted in their school, and they translated their dream into goals and expectations for teachers and students by establishing important curricular programs. At each step along the way, they received encouragement and active involvement from administrators. Public communication received constant attention as well: China Day and the "Parade of Nations" information fair galvanized community interest and involvement. Early on, the help of the parent-teacher association was sought in planning these events; in this way the need of parents to stay informed and assist in school improvement was satisfied.

Joshua Eaton teachers took their message of professional growth and change to other teachers and schools in Reading and beyond. The Peabody Museum, Children's Museum, MGEP and other groups helped with material resources, speakers, and classroom-ready activities. In the end, the Eaton team received an institutional commitment to the process of change from the school system.

"Our objective is global peace," said Nicklasson. "At a young age our students have become aware of children in other parts of the globe; of the similarities of their play and their hopes and dreams. This common understanding and hope for the future promotes perspective taking and an interest in the cultures of others."

Global education is often a goal in itself. Such is the case when a school commits itself to broadening its pupils' contacts with non-Western cultures or when a school faculty consciously tries to add another world view to its social studies curriculum.

Now that the project has been under way for some time, we can reflect upon things we have learned. Most important, it would seem, is the fact that global education can serve as a vehicle for school renewal. There is no doubt but that the morale of the faculty at Joshua Eaton is now extremely high. The pride and enthusiasm can be seen not only in special programs such as the art exchange with the Pei Zheng Elementary School in China, the Massachusetts and the World project and the Parade of Nations information fair, but in the day-to-day business of schooling.

School renewal at Joshua Eaton is also manifested in an improved curriculum and classroom instructional practice. The formation of the school-wide advisory committee with the task of finding ways to globalize the curriculum is evidence of this, as are the many and varied teaching units which continue to be developed and field-tested by individual teachers.

A second important lesson learned from this project was that individual schools can benefit greatly from being connected to outside agencies which have the knowledge that they need. Not only did the Joshua Eaton faculty benefit from their affiliation with MGEP, but they also were brought into contact with the Principals' Center at the Harvard Graduate School of Education, the Massachusetts Geography Alliance, Salem State College, the Peabody Museum, Educators' for Social Responsibility (ESR), and other agencies. Such networking serves as a vehicle for keeping teachers aware of important new ideas and developments.

Finally, an important step in the innovation process is that of institutionalization. This is a step which does not always occur in school-based global education projects, but it seems to have occurred at Joshua Eaton. Teachers from the school were actually invited to be part of district-wide planning because of their program. The superintendent and assistant superintendent both endorsed the work done at the school and, in fact, the initial charge to the faculty to globalize came from then-assistant superintendent Robert Munelly.

The faculty at Joshua Eaton Elementary chose to make global education a cornerstone of their efforts to improve their school's curriculum and instruction. In so doing, they gave their students dynamic and challenging courses of study. The scale and scope of activity at Joshua Eaton is impressive. Certainly, they have made a good beginning and, at this writing, it appears as if they will continue the development of an innovative globalized curriculum.

NOTES

1. Harlan Cleveland, speech given at the *American Forum Conference on Education and International Competence*, St. Louis, Missouri, May 15, 1988.

CHAPTER FIVE

TUFFREE JUNIOR HIGH

Ida Urso

   Tuffree Junior High school, located in Orange County just 20 miles southeast of Los Angeles, is a suburban 7-8 school within a homogeneous, white upper-middle class neighborhood. To broaden the students' horizons, in 1987, two teachers began taking groups of students—with parent chaperones—on a "Walk Through the Real World" in downtown Los Angeles. There the students witnessed the shocking contrasts between high-tech architecture and affluence, and abject poverty and homelessness. They also visited various ethnic enclaves—Little Tokyo, Chinatown, and Olvera Street, site of the original Hispanic settlement that eventually became the city of Los Angeles.
   The "Real World" walk is just one of the eye-opening activities Tuffree students have participated in during the school's four-year association with the Center for Human Interdependence (CHI) of Chapman College in Orange, California. Over the past four years, Tuffree has been one of eleven schools belonging to CHI's "global education network." Being a network school has meant that the district, the principal, and a significant number of teachers at the school have shown an interest in working with CHI to introduce global awareness into the curriculum of the school. In return, CHI has provided a variety of resources and services: a comprehensive curriculum library, workshops and conferences on various international issues,

mini-grants for the development of global lessons, and quarterly newsletters, to name just a few.

Placentia, the city in which Tuffree Junior High is located, is approximately 90 percent Anglo, with 65 percent of the families reporting an annual income of more than $40,000. There are 630 students at Tuffree and 25 teachers. The school also has one psychologist, one mentor teacher, and two counselors.

Although Anglo students form the vast majority (83 percent), Hispanic students make up 9 percent of the student body. Asians comprise 6 percent, blacks one percent and there is an additional one percent from a variety of other ethnic groups. The ethnic representation is not as diverse among teachers, of whom 94 percent are Anglo, 3 percent are black and 3 percent are Asian. Interestingly, this homogeneity played a significant role in the globalization of the curriculum at Tuffree. Because of it, several teachers and the principal believed strongly that their students needed a better understanding of the world beyond their immediate neighborhood.

FERTILE GROUND FOR A GLOBAL PERSPECTIVE

From the very beginning, CHI was deliberately general and non-specific regarding the goals it wanted to achieve with Tuffree. The CHI staff believed that such nondirectedness would enhance the teachers' creativity, moltivation, and feelings of ownership of the project; and so it was. During the four years of the project, the "Tuffree tribe" (a name assigned to the school by its teachers) always outdid itself. The teachers there took pride in continuously challenging themselves to do better.

Along with the principal, six teachers representing special education, reading, language arts, music, social studies and mathematics participated in the first meeting at Tuffree with CHI. One teacher at this meeting told the CHI representatives that he and another colleague had "thrown out the district curriculum" and designed a high-interest program which included all of the district requirements, but which was much more relevant for the students.

Another teacher at that meeting was described in the field notes as having an "absolute enthusiasm for global education." She believed that "...if a teacher really wants to prepare his or her students for the 21st century, then he or she must teach the students everything from a global perspective, no matter what the subject."

At this first meeting, CHI was also invited to an "international breakfast" which was organized by the social studies, music, science, math, art, home economics, and physical education teachers. Students, dressed in ethnic costumes from around the world, served the faculty and guests an assortment of foods from other cultures.

Teacher Bill Melvin summed up the CHI effect on Tuffree: "The interest in global education had been simmering for years. It burst open when contact was made with CHI." From CHI's vantage point, looking back on what made the work at Tuffree so successful, a theme seems to stand out, one which is especially interesting. It has been labeled *conditions for engagement.*

In a preliminary assessment of the interaction with Tuffree, Ken Tye, co-director of CHI, wrote in an in-house memo "...We have had a remarkably positive reception and a number of successes at Tuffree." Tye enumerated four conditions which led to this early success:

1. Support for global education and futures studies at the district level. The Placentia Unifed School District superintendent, Dr. Keith Larick, taught a futures course at a local college. The district agreed to provide 10-15 days of release time per year for four years, so that Tuffree teachers would be able to attend workshops and other events organized by CHI.

2. Similar support from the principal, Dick Vouga, plus an interest on his part in developing a truly distinctive

school. Vouga indicated that the purpose of CHI was consistent with his own philosophy.

3. Prior interest in and valuing of "global" or "international" education—"international" being principal Vouga's preferred term in the early years of this project, because of his wish to avoid any problems with conservative members of the community who might object to the idea of "global" education.

4. A significant group of interested teachers who, for a variety of reasons, saw this project as fitting in nicely with their own interests and goals.

DISTRICT-LEVEL SUPPORT

These "conditions for engagement" deserve closer scrutiny. Except for a once-a-year meeting, there was not much formal interaction between CHI and the school district. This annual meeting, however, had a dual purpose: first, the CHI staff and the Tuffree principal reported on the global education activities of the year just ending and, second, the district promised release days for teachers to use in global education planning during the year ahead. The reports to district administrators included details such as (1) the number of contacts made with teachers at the school; (2) teacher attendance at CHI workshops and conferences; (3) mini-grant applications and information about grants awarded at the school that year; (4) materials requested and used by teachers at the school; and (5) any special programs carried out at the school. When all forms of contact were totaled like this, it was generally impressive.

Although formal interaction with the district office was infrequent, the importance of district support cannot be minimized. Having such backing legitimized the CHI project in the eyes of the principal, his staff, and the community; it sent the message to the faculty members that they were free to establish their own relationship with CHI.

It has been said that formal CHI contact with the district was limited. However, it should be noted that there was significant *informal* contact with many district-level administrators from all of the districts having schools involved in the CHI network through professional association activities, Orange County Office of Education meetings, and so forth. CHI staff members were well known to local school district administrators.

PRINCIPAL SUPPORT

Dick Vouga, the principal at the outset of CHI's involvement with Tuffree, had a genuine interest in global education. His readiness for the project was evident from the start. Having listened to CHI's intention to help interested teachers globalize their curriculum, Vouga asked, "Well, what's our next step? When do we get started? How do we get consultants out here, and workshops going? We want our people trained ASAP!"

Two years later, in a reflective interview with Ken Tye, Vouga referred to aspects of the CHI project in these terms: "The initial steps were healthy. CHI's work with small groups was appreciated. There was no initial resistance because CHI did not seek to thrust the project on the whole faculty. The single-day inservices were significant for the teachers as it gave them a chance to get out of school and to network with other interested teachers. And the small grants given really encouraged the teachers to produce units they actually would use in their classes." Vouga, who was being transferred to another intermediate school, said that he intended to tell his new faculty that "...global education is the nature of middle-level education." Expressing his appreciation, Vouga added, "CHI came in as a service—not another demand. A lot of projects say they are going to do that; CHI actually did it."

George Bowman, who replaced Vouga as principal at Tuffree at the beginning of the third year of the CHI network project, continued to support the ongoing global education activities. In speaking about the new principal, one of the teachers said "George is very supportive. He is a real doer. That's a great strength. He will do battle for whatever he believes is appropriate and correct, no matter who objects." Bowman's support can be seen through his attendance at various CHI activities outside of the Tuffree campus, as well as his involvement in the many global education projects which took place at the school.

The support of both principals, their interest in global awareness, and their intent to develop a truly distinctive school made a fruitful relationship between CHI and Tuffree possible.

RECEPTIVITY OF TEACHERS

At an early faculty meeting at Tuffree attended by CHI staff, teachers were asked to fill out a questionnaire so that the needs, interests, and expertise of the Tuffree faculty would be better understood. The first question asked teachers to note which ideas regarding global perspectives they would like to pursue with their students. The variety and sophistication of responses to this question indicated that a significant segment of the staff was open to some form of global awareness education at Tuffree. Also, it is important to note that out of a staff of 25 teachers, 19 responded to the questionnaire. Thus, most of the teachers were predisposed to bringing a global perspective into their classrooms.

The first faculty meeting to which CHI was invited was the international breakfast mentioned earlier. At this event, the teachers and students who cooked and served the breakfast were in colorful ethnic dress. Tables were decorated with flags and artifacts to reflect the cultures found on the six inhabited continents of the world. A huge sign reading "International Perspectives" was placed in front of the speakers' podium. The honors students gave all the teachers a "World Citizen Quiz," graded it, and announced the highest scores at this breakfast. Three of the teachers spoke to their colleagues, emphasizing the need to incorporate an international perspective into the school curriculum. One of them gave a short presentation on how each department could teach from an international perspective.

THE POWER OF A SHARED VISION

At Tuffree, the conditions for global education were clearly opportune. It helped, too, as both principals and other teachers mentioned, that no one on the staff was opposed to the inclusion of global perspectives in the curriculum. A major key to the success of global education at Tuffree comes from the power of a shared vision. This "shared vision" idea provides an explanation for, and insight into, many of CHI's experiences at Tuffree. The program was led by Bill Melvin, Jim Perry, and Rubin White, three dynamic, caring, concerned and energetic teachers who wanted to make their school the best that it could be, and to meet the needs of their students and the community in the process. These three teachers and their principal shared a belief in the importance of providing relevant global awareness education experiences both for the students and for the community. When coupled with the CHI staff and resources, these educators provided the right mix, wielded the right amount of influence and infected other teachers with their enthusiasm and vision to a degree that made a great variety of creative programs at the school possible.

These key players had a history of working in a cooperative and interdisciplinary manner at Tuffree. In fact, the 7th grade teachers had been planning a core class interweaving different disciplines including reading, English, geography, and transitional skills. The core program went into effect the second year of CHI involvement. The center of the core was the social studies, and social studies, as these teachers saw it, had to include global perspectives.

In various conversations with CHI staff, the key teachers said that because of their involvement with the project, they no longer felt isolated in their efforts but, rather, they felt even more encouraged to make the changes they deemed necessary. One indicated that before the project came to Tuffree, 20-30% of the staff had any interest in global perspectives. During the fourth year of the project, according to this teacher, 80-90% expressed a great interest in the concept and were working to bring global awareness more thoroughly into their teaching.

WHO "OWNS" GLOBAL EDUCATION?

In the second year of the project, CHI staff members became concerned that this group of key teachers was laying claim to the project and that in spite of their very fine work, their "ownership" was causing other teachers to shy away. For this reason, Ken Tye met with principal Vouga and they, together, designed a small study. A sample of teachers was interviewed. Included in the sample were active participants as well as teachers who had not participated.

What was found was that things were perceived as being channeled through the "core" group by the principal. The people in the 7th grade core group—the key teachers referred to earlier—were well-liked and respected, but there was some resentment and a few people felt shut out. For their part, the core group did acknowledge getting a lot of satisfaction from their involvement, and they saw that it would be helpful if they would reach out more to include their colleagues.

Everyone who was interviewed, regardless of their level of personal involvement with CHI, was positive about global education and the project. They also were very pleased with having the opportunity to express themselves through the interviews. A feedback session was scheduled and, as a result, a pledge was made to encourage broader participation.

SPECIAL TUFFREE PROJECTS

At the end of the third year, one teacher stated that CHI had been a "positive plus" for the school, and that teachers felt a sense of power and creativity as a result of their work with global education. This power and creativity is evident in a number of dynamic and innovative projects designed by the teachers at Tuffree and affecting the students and the community during the time period from early 1986 to June of 1989. Seven of these projects are highlighted below. At the heart of each one stands one or more key teachers and the principal, plus some kind of support from CHI in all cases but one.

1. **"Walk Through the Real World,"** organized by Bill Melvin and Jim Perry and assisted by two other teachers in 1986, 1987, and 1989. Through the analysis of a previous sociology unit of study, it became apparent to the teachers that the students had no awareness of their own greater community, let alone the world. "The idea was formed to help students gain a better awareness and understanding, and CHI made it possible," said Perry.

The students, with a few of the parents, were taken through a five-mile walking tour of "the best and the worst of downtown L.A." The itinerary included a visit to the upscale, futuristic Bonaventure Hotel; seedy Main Street; bustling Broadway; Little Tokyo and Chinatown; Olvera Street for a taste of Mexico; and a visit to the Fred Jordon Mission which houses and feeds the homeless. As "junior sociologists," the students were to study the city and that same evening write recommendations to L.A. Mayor Tom Bradley about how they thought the city should be improved. Since Tuffree teacher Rubin White had had the opportunity to be in committee meetings with the mayor, she passed these reports on to him, and he graciously read and responded to them. The students' impressions of their experiences were varied:

> "I just thought everybody had houses and cars and things like that, but it was really sad." "At first I thought they were all weird, but when I saw the man in the park living in a cardboard box, I was really bothered."
>
> "Dear Mayor Bradley, you've got problems. Can't you do something to help these people?"
>
> "Thank you Mr. Melvin and Mr. Perry. I never could have learned about this in class."
>
> "It was so nice at the hotel and then it got so dirty just down the street. It was awful." "It was the best thing that I ever did at Tuffree."

2. **Anthropology Night.** Organized by Melvin with the help of Perry, White, the principal, Larry Butler and the students and held annually in the fall since 1983. Only parents are invited (without their children). The intent of this event is to help build community, to give parents a taste of what their children are learning in school, and to educate the parents. The focus of the evening is on Africa. Since Tuffree's involvement with CHI, Melvin and Perry have concentrated on teaching activities that help build cross-cultural awareness. The parents are also given an outline of what the students will be studying the whole year, including the time line of each unit. This evening usually brings out 80 to 90 parents, and CHI was told that "...it gets more positive feedback than anything else at the school."

3. **World War II Night.** Organized by Perry with the help of Melvin, White, and the principal. It has been held four times in the spring since 1983, once with helping funds from CHI. All parents are invited. The intent of this program is similar to that of Anthropology Night. This time, the parents take a "moral look at war." Once again, as in the above activity, parents become students and are exposed to a global theme.

4. Welcome to Our World. Organized by Melvin, Perry White, Jerry Bader, Doug Thompson, Harv Callaghan and principal Bowman. It was an evening program for parents, students, and the community held in the spring of 1989. This program was written as a mini-grant proposal which CHI funded. The intent was "to develop a global program, involving multidisciplinary cooperation and, ultimately, to publish a folklore magazine and a how-to manual on producing global education projects. The event was a huge success, with capacity crowds on both nights that it was held. Bill Melvin began the evening by telling the audience that at Tuffree, nearly 35 countries of the world are represented. These countries were starred on a world map strategically placed in the entrance to the school. Bill then read a handout provided by the CHI office entitled "Our American Citizen," indicating how many of our day-to-day living habits connect us to all parts of the world through the foods we eat, clothes we wear, and materials we use.

Folk plays from India and Japan were then performed by the students, after which the audience went to any three of five "breakout rooms," where they saw an ethnic style show; heard original literary presentations on global issues; took a global knowledge test; experienced an intimate area study of the land and people of Guatemala; or browsed in a room full of student art, global artifacts and global information. The formal evening program ended with songs written and performed by the students, folkdancing from the Middle East, South Africa, and Austria, and ethnic refreshments.

5. Fate of the Forest. Organized by Melvin, Perry, White, Butler, Bowman and Jerry Bader in the spring of 1987. Financial support for this program came from a National Science Foundation grant. The purposes of this evening program for the students, parents, and the community at large were to educate everyone about the fate of the forests of the world; show students that they can make a difference; and raise funds for the World Wildlife Fund. The audience was broken into groups and asked to solve a problem from the perspective of various segments of society affected by the destruction or saving of the world's forests.

6. **International Sports Awareness Day.** Spring 1987, 1988, and 1989. The first two years were organized by the 7th grade physical education teachers, particularly Cindy Watson and Nancy Landau, in cooperation with other teachers working with CHI. Because these events were so tremendously popular, in 1989 five teachers and principal Bowman set up the event for *all* students and interested teachers at Tuffree. The intent of the day was to familiarize students with non-competitive games played by children in other cultures of the world.

7. **World Outline Map.** Tuffree teacher Liz Greenhill applied for a mini-grant in 1987 to have a large world outline map painted on the outdoor quad area of the school grounds to be used as a visual and learning aid by classes at the school. It has since been used to teach locations and cultures in geography, ecological zones in science, world literature and story settings in reading, and food and dress in home economics.

CONCLUDING THOUGHTS

Many teachers other than the core group have been involved in global education activities. Attendance at CHI workshops, a wide range of materials checked out from the CHI curriculum library, and classroom visitations attest to this.

A number of important things have been learned as a result of the four exciting years of CHI involvement with Tuffree. A critical one has been that what CHI staff members came to think of as "conditions for engagement" have to be favorable. At Tuffree there was a supportive superintendent, ready to commit precious release-time days for teacher inservice. There was a principal interested in global education and flexible enough to make adjustments as necessary. There was a group of respected teachers, willing to work hard to develop and implement programs and to reach out to involve their colleagues.

A second learning was that it is important to have a continuing support mechanism such as CHI. What Barbara Benham Tye has called the "deep structure" of schooling is so powerful that it is probably true that a school cannot maintain its innovative impetus without some form of external support—financial, material, psychological—and link to new knowledge and ideas. (1)

A third thing learned was that caution must be taken to avoid having a global education initiative become the sole property of a small group of hard-working, well-meaning "early adopters" who, without intending to, effectively cut off the rest of the faculty from becoming involved.

A final learning was that the "organization development people" are correct: gathering data and giving feedback as to the results, *to the people from whom the data were collected,* is a viable improvement strategy which can be used in schools to further the cause of global education.

Certainly, in the years to come, the core group at Tuffree will continue to bring a global perspective to their curricula. The degree to which global awareness will remain as a focus for the whole school is not known, however. CHI's formal involvement ended with the 1988-89 school year. The district and the current principal have other priorities. It will be interesting to return to Tuffree in several years and see what is happening. Perhaps they still will be "walking in the real world."

NOTES

1. Barbara Benham Tye. "The Deep Structure of Schooling," *Phi Delta Kappan,* 69: 281-83, December, 1987.

CHAPTER SIX

NORTHEAST MAGNET SCHOOL

David Gidich

Less than 20 miles west of the United Nations lives a group of people working to promote peace and understanding among different nations through their elementary school. The teachers at the Northeast "International Studies" Magnet School believe strongly in promoting cultural and global awareness through education.

The Northeast School is located in Montclair Township in Essex County, New Jersey. Montclair's population of nearly 40,000 is 67 percent white, 29 percent black, and two percent each Asian and Hispanic. The town is made up of three unofficial but politically and socially recognized regions: the southern, central, and northern areas. Most of the blacks and Hispanics live in the southern and central sections.

Montclair's houses were recently described by *New Jersey Magazine* as "ranging from $175,000 to $2.2 million, and nearly all are on smallish lots and pretty, tree-lined streets. An average home is 65 years old and costs about $300,000."

The Montclair Public School District, serving a student population of 1,700, has effectively operated with an approved desegregation plan since 1972. Six elementary and two middle schools are desegregated through a voluntary busing plan called "Freedom of Choice."

The Northeast School is located in the northeastern corner of town, known as "Upper Montclair" by the residents. This northernmost section surrounding the school has some of the town's most expensive single-family homes. Nearly one-third of the school's student body lives in this section; more than two-thirds of the school's 350 students live more than one mile from the school and are bused.

Under the leadership of superintendent Dr. Mary Lee Fitzgerald, in May 1985, the Montclair Board of Education applied for federal funds to modify and expand the Freedom of Choice Program. These funds permitted plans for the development of the Northeast Magnet School to proceed.

Northeast School, a 54-year-old, two-story stone structure, was designated a magnet school, joining five other Montclair magnet programs. In 1975, two gifted-and-talented schools and a math/reading fundamental magnet were created; an arts institute fundamental magnet was started in 1980; and in 1982, a science/technology school was begun.

Northeast has had a long tradition of academic excellence. Many of its graduates have been sought-after by the various middle schools in the district because of this tradition and, indeed, for decades realtors have used the reputation of the school as an enticement when selling homes in the area. In recent years, this has become a problem since Northeast is no longer a neighborhood school and new home buyers ultimately find out that their children are not guaranteed enrollment there.

THE ORIGINAL IMPETUS

Since it was the last neighborhood school in the district, some students prior to 1985 were being attracted from the Northeast section to Montclair's other strongly-marketed magnet programs. It became essential that Northeast create a program which would generate its own "magnetism" and compete with the attraction of the other magnet programs.

This was the challenge for the Northeast Planning Committee. (It is interesting to note that at this writing, five years after Northeast became a magnet, this year there have been fewer than a dozen transfers in and about the same number attend other schools).

The impetus for Northeast's "International Studies" magnet was the already existing culturally diverse population of ESL children at the school. Even before the magnet, all ESL students were at Northeast. In 1989, there were 42 students from 25 countries, speaking 18 different languages.

But the International Studies Magnet could not be started up the same way the other Montclair magnets had been. The planning model of the mid-1970s, which involved a team whose sole, year-long effort was to develop a proposal, could no longer be financially supported. Federal money had waned, and new funding had to be found. The tax burden for continuing "Freedom of Choice" shifted to the local property owner. Skyrocketing local property taxes tempered planning efforts and program designs. Knowing that the community's support for raising taxes was not strong, particularly since the largest expense for the magnet program was busing, a team of Northeast teachers, parents, and administrators got together with consultants from two groups: Global Education, Inc., a New Jersey-based educational consultant group; and the Experiment in International Living, a Vermont program specializing in international education. This team went on "retreat" for one week at the Experiment headquarters in Brattleboro, Vermont. There, led by the Northeast School principal and the Director of Global Education, Inc., they learned to work together as a team and they developed a set of themes to be used to guide the school in its subsequent program development. Briefly, those themes were: cooperation; multicultural tolerance and appreciation; development of a global view, particularly as that relates to conservation and ecology; and foreign language proficiency. The team returned to Montclair full of enthusiasm.

GETTING UNDER WAY

In the late spring of 1985, a series of planning meetings were conducted. It was hoped that the new magnet would actively contribute to the district's desegregation effort by attracting and maintaining a racially and sexually integrated population. The planners envisioned students who would better grasp the importance of cultural and global awareness, while creatively and peacefully solving problems and resolving conflicts. Additionally, the desire to expose learners to a second language led to the development of a partial-immersion foreign language experience.

Plans begun in the summer of 1985 were carried through during the fall, and culminated in the presentation of a proposal to the Board of Education in the spring of 1986. The proposal was within district financial and programmatic boundaries. It embedded "International Studies" activities within the pre-existing social studies curriculum and infused a foreign language component into art and music classes. This gave the ESL students a special chance to "shine."

Shortly thereafter, the Board of Education adopted the following statement of objectives:

> By designating Northeast International Elementary School a magnet program and by offering its students enhancements of the adopted social studies curriculum and foreign language immersion experiences, it is expected that (1) a racially and sexually integrated student population will be attracted and maintained at each grade level; (2) students will demonstrate an appreciation of the similarities and diversities of human culture; (3) students will evidence an awareness of alternative means of communicating; (4) students will demonstrate knowledge of world trends and issues, and the interconnection of such trends and issues to the students' lives; (5) students will develop problem-solving and conflict resolution skills so that they may exert influence and resolve/manage conflicts; and (6) a district-wide public information program will be presented to inquiring parents and interested community members.

THE PROGRAM

At each level, from pre-kindergarten to fifth grade, units emphasizing "international studies" program objectives were devised. In the fourth grade, where students received 45 minutes of social studies instruction daily emphasizing New Jersey history, commerce, and cultural development, students now view New Jersey's links to other parts of the world. One unit challenged learners to identify how inventions developed in New Jersey were applied throughout the world. In kindergarten, the childrens' cultural heritage was featured as their parents addressed the class using cultural artifacts, stories, poems, traditional dress, and representative foods. Fifth grade students learned the value of cooperation as they respond to a "new games" physical education dilemma which emphasized the value of cooperation over competition. In December, the tradition at Northeast has been to have a holiday sing. Since the advent of the International Studies Magnet, activities have included such events as a peace festival, and a play celebrating holiday traditions around the world.

Foreign language offerings in the magnets are designed to be unique and not duplicate other programs. Northeast's choice of a foreign language was Spanish. A partial-immersion experience in foreign language was designed, since another magnet already had an elective, pull-out program. The foreign language classes at Northeast offer students the chance to develop an "ear" for vocabulary and expressions in the hope that, as middle school students, they will continue to study Spanish.

Each year the students enter Northeast School after their parents view the six distinct magnet programs. The ability to continue to attract sufficient numbers of students is the primary testament of the school's effectiveness, since parents and students are free to "vote with their feet" if they are unhappy with the school. A formal review of the program's objectives is conducted each year through the

School Review Council. This advisory committee to the superintendent establishes, reviews, and reports on the progress of the school.

The 1988-89 year ended with each grade level in the International Studies Magnet exploring an assigned continent. The studies included cultural, geographic, economic, religious and political investigations and projects. The school hallways became showcases for the work done by the students. In 1989-90, each grade established a relationship with a school on "their" continent, and letters and video messages were exchanged. Thus far, the Northeast school has a sister school in Ghana.

PROBLEMS SOLVED AND LESSONS LEARNED

Through a state "Partners in Learning" grant, Northeast School has been able to use the services of Global Learning, inc. staff to help with ongoing planning. Once a month, on a Thursday, students have been released at 1:00 pm and teachers have worked together to plan classroom learning activities and to learn about global issues. At the end of the 1988-89 school year, a new, sizeable federal grant was allocated to the Montclair Schools to update their magnet schools program. As a result, at this writing, the faculty is considering what direction that program should take in the future.

There have been some problems along the way. The first has to do with test scores. A majority of the faculty have been together at Northeast for many years. They have been proud of the reputation the school has gained for its academic excellence. For years, Northeast has had the best test scores in the district. Tests do not necessarily measure the outcomes of the global education program and, while scores have remained good, they have not been quite as high in the past few years.

In addition, while teachers in general, have been supportive of the global education program, they have recently felt the pressure of competing demands. Besides the focus on test scores having to do with basic skills, there are such other things as a new family-life curriculum and a growing number of ESL students.

Faculty attrition has also put stress on the program. The principal was reassigned at the end of the 1988-89 school year. So was the bilingual music teacher, Ann Marie Flores. The art teacher, Joan Jasterzbski, took maternity leave. The core of the global education program had been the team of Flores, Jasterzbski, and the bilingual ESL teacher, Marty Miller.

A number of lessons have been learned from this experience. The availability of outside resources such as those provided by Global Education, Inc. was very important. So was the inservice training provided by the Brattleboro retreat, and the monthly early-release days. On the other hand, because this was a mandated program and because teachers were not involved in thorough discussion of the purposes of schooling and/or the specific objectives of Northeast School, a confusion remained between the priorities for basic skills on the one hand and global education on the other. The reality is that the two need not be in conflict, but this was not clarified as well as was needed initially.

Related to the latter concern is the fact that a great deal of hope was invested in a small core of teachers. As good as those people were, when many of them left, the program was threatened. Any innovative program has much more chance of long-term success when participation is widespread.

Thus far, students have shown a willingness to be open to different ideas, sounds, tastes, and views of life. They have come to realize that the world is a shrinking place and needs to be cared for. What will happen to the program remains to be seen. Given today's world, one must hope that it will continue to flourish as it has since 1985.

CHAPTER SEVEN

ELAINE HIGH SCHOOL

Jennifer Shumaker

Here's a challenge. Imagine this school setting: a group of students boycott classes in support of making Martin Luther King's birthday a holiday. The global studies club earns money to pay for a lengthy bus ride to learn about small farms, and then raises funds for poor farmers around the world. Later, the club organizes an International Day.

Surely, this must be a group of comfortable cosmopolitan kids, who know the power of protest in the United States and whose parents support their endeavors.

Wrong.

Beneath the promising recent achievements of this global studies club lies an impoverished, racially segregated small town. The community itself is but one of the many obstacles its poor children must overcome. But due to the courage of two brave teachers and numerous students, the door has been flung open to a much more promising future.

Welcome to "the other America," to Elaine, Arkansas; population 1,300. You leave Highway 40 in eastern Arkansas halfway between Memphis and Little Rock, and enter the Delta—the area of large farms and rapidly deteriorating rural towns. Entering Elaine, the first building visible is a large farm implement dealership, then a "Jesus heals both heart and home" billboard. You pass another farm supply store, a small church, and a series of dilapidated green shacks. A small black child plays in the yard of one;

an old man rocks on a chair outside another. Now on to the center of town, with the usual general stores and an unusually elaborate new building—the *white* Southern Baptist Church.

After the large church, we cross the ditch that separates Elaine's whites from her blacks. This street leading to the high school may be the only part of the white residential area many of the blacks ever see, and this they can do only after school while they walk straight without stopping until they get back into the black area across "the ditch."

Most of the whites in Elaine are connected to farming, either as farmers or farm suppliers. Others hold virtually all available jobs in the banks, stores, and other community positions. The black people either work and live on the farms as laborers, hold more menial public service positions, or survive on welfare in the little shacks across the ditch.

Recently, for the first time, Elaine residents elected a black to the City Council. Since Elaine is 70% white, some white people must have voted for Leester Garner, who has brought about some changes and hopes for more. With the new, young mayor who is attempting to bring in some housing reforms, perhaps the black area of town will change. Leester is disappointed right now because after voting to install running water and gas in the little green shacks, the City Council now wants to charge the residents of the shacks for hook-ups.

Elaine High School, with 500 students in grades 9 through 12, is a sparkling new building located south of the white area of town.

Although the town is about 70 percent white, only 15 percent of the high school students are white. Most white parents send their children to a local academy or a private school. The public schools are left to provide a modest education, often just barely enough to remain accredited.

Many of the 22 teachers have been at the school for more than 15 years, principal Lucien Webster is proud to relate. About a third of the teachers are black, but all the new teachers hired recently have been white, and it is hard to ignore the whiteness of the administration—every one, even the secretaries, is white in this mostly black school.

According to Webster, there has been a steady stream of young teachers who have come to Elaine High, but who have left after a short while. Webster explains that these are mostly the math and foreign language instructors who come for a little experience. "Elaine is an ideal place for beginning teachers to get their feet wet," he said. Some teachers tell a different story: new arrivals must either adjust to community values or leave. This means deciding to accept the racial divisions or risk their jobs by challenging the status quo.

Elaine High School, like many rural Arkansas schools, offers little more than is required to remain accredited. But since Arkansas launched new school standards a few years ago, many changes have taken place. The school now offers band, Spanish, career development and global studies. Another drastic change was brought about by the requirement that every eighth grader pass a standardized test before entering high school. Recently, Elaine was embarrassed when only 56 percent of the eighth graders passed the test on the first try. Only one other school in the entire state scored lower. To make matters worse, the high school in the town of Lakeview next door, with totally black enrollment, black administration and only one white faculty member, boasted 100 percent passing on the first test.

The new requirements also mandated that all Arkansas high schools offer global studies, so in the fall of 1985, Webster sent social studies teacher Billie McCray to a workshop at the local community college. Seeing it as a punitive chore, McCray was less than enthusiastic about her newly-assigned task.

TWO PIVOTAL PEOPLE

Billie McCray is a black woman in her 30s, with the unmistakable calm strength of someone fulfilling a purpose.

She has lived most of her life in the farming area near Elaine. But unlike most people with similar backgrounds, McCray doesn't share the seemingly predominant feeling of helplessness about the fate of black children in this rural town.

So Miss Billie, as she is known in the community, reluctantly attended the workshop. For her, the turning point came on the fourth day when McCray encountered George Otero, from the Las Palomas de Taos Education Retreat Center in New Mexico. He shared his enthusiasm and approach to teaching global education in a series of breakout sessions. McCray recalls how Otero spoke of the students; how he said "They are going to inherit the world." She thought to herself, "This is what *my* kids need."

"I always thought I was in a world by myself," said McCray. "Here I was screaming and shouting and hollering about things, without much to back me up. Suddenly, I found a lot of great people who shared my feelings." Otero recommended that McCray find someone else at Elaine to "jump off the cliff" with her, and McCray knew that had to be her "fellow agitator," English teacher Shirley Larry. Likewise regarded as a strong woman, Larry's latest controversy concerned an assignment she gave her class: the black kids were to write about how it must have felt to be slave owners, and the white kids were to write about how it felt to be slaves. A black parent reported to Elaine Schools Superintendent Kenneth Parker that Larry was trying to stir up racism. This sort of experience, the parent said, could potentially arouse the hatred he had felt while watching the television series "Roots." He said that he hadn't been previously aware that his ancestors were slaves.

Shirley Larry tried to explain to him that his hatred was a result of his lack of education. She told him she would rather the kids learn to live with the truth than hide in Elaine with a lie.

So together, Larry and McCray, armed with workshop materials, went to work. They studied the games, the simulations, the debates, and decided to use this fresh, no-textbook, team teaching approach in all their classes. McCray's government class staged debates and mock trials and Larry's journalism class reported on them. Teaching without texts required far more student participation, and both students and teachers were rejuvenated.

Forty-five students attended the first global studies class, and a club was formed. They named the club "GIG," for Global Insights Gained, and began a series of "Global Raps." Since the class was assigned to students who were potential troublemakers, the teachers ended up with the "challenging" students. "They stuck all the kids in there that the white teachers couldn't handle," laughed McCray. "So we got the lively black kids, special education kids, and really smart kids—the kinds of students I love to work with. They challenged me and I challenged them."

Additionally, the class was filled with football players. It is reportedly a common practice in some Arkansas districts to place football players into special education classes, to ensure passing grades.

GIG took off like wildfire. Full of popular athletes, lively misfits, and bright, inquisitive students, they quickly chose their leaders, decided on their goals, wrote their constitution, and went to work.

GIG CHANGES THE SYSTEM

Several of McCray's students, including Lee Campbell, Ronald Hall and Lee Hall, were responsible for a student boycott of school in protest of the lack of a Martin Luther King holiday. The week prior to King's birthday, Campbell and a group of students asked principal Webster if the school could have the day off. Webster refused, saying that the holidays had been set at the beginning of the school year, and that *that* was the time to request a holiday. The students had a petition with many signatures, and warned the principal that if they couldn't get the day off, they would boycott school on King's birthday, the following Monday.

Two days later, McCray looked out of the office window and remarked to the secretary, "Hey, there's a camera out there!" Suddenly, she remembered that Hall had asked her how to go about contacting a Little Rock TV station.

Webster was furious. Students were holding protest signs outside, and the TV cameras captured it all. Webster called the students "stupid" and yelled at the cameraman. When a coach ordered the kids to put the signs down, Ronald Hall turned to McCray and asked, "Miss McCray, you told us in the classroom that everyone has the right to protest." McCray concurred, and the students continued their demonstration, with the camera taping it all.

Only 28 students (out of 500) showed up at school on King's birthday, and a group of black parents later put in a strong enough request that the school board granted the holiday off in succeeding years. The global studies club had stirred up a controversy, and had successfully changed the district policy in honoring King.

LINKS TO THE OUTSIDE WORLD

For McCray and Larry, most of the excitement of the new global studies program stemmed from the opportunity to show the students a whole different world that was available to them outside of their small Southern town. "Interdependence is the theme that impressed me the most," said McCray. "Our superintendent has said that what happens in Elaine has no bearing on the outside world, and what happens in the outside world has no bearing on Elaine. But I saw global studies as a way of teaching these kids that our community *is* connected to other places. We *are* interdependent."

"I want to teach my kids that they are entitled to their own opinions—that there are not necessarily any right answers to some things. Sometimes there are different answers and sometimes you won't even find an answer. Sometimes we can just play with a problem and it just won't have a simple solution."

"Values also intrigue me: our kids are so wrapped up in the system. I see values as a way of bringing different things back into the classroom and to talk about values in other places. By doing this, I can bring in different cultures, and explain how it is good to understand differences and similarities. People don't have to be alike and just because some people are different, it doesn't mean they are wrong and we should look down on them. We should be able to understand and appreciate these differences in the world and then work together as people."

"Before Global Studies, I really didn't have a standardized way of bringing this to them. I could say it, and give examples, but Global Studies has given me themes, good examples, materials from the workshops; all these."

GIG members became intent on finding out about life outside of Elaine. The students voted to charge a $5 membership fee to use for field trips. That first year, they drove to Little Rock, to Memphis, and to the Heifer Project International, a non-profit small farmers support organization in Perryville, Arkansas. The GIG kids, who came from some of the poorest families in America, returned from the Heifer Project visit and raised $300 for poor farmers around the world.

The club then brought Father Jaime Diez, the former director of the Colombian International Curriculum Development for Rural Schools, to their school. The global studies class wrote essays about the visit:

> "The thing I will remember most about Señor Diez is he is willing to take on other people's problems," wrote one student. "When we discussed teenage pregnancy, someone said the problem did not concern her, but Reverend Diez said we must concern ourselves with others' problems because they may someday be our own. I say we must stop being narrow-minded, for there is a whole world outside of this shanty town."

"My thoughts on Latin America changed," wrote another student. "I had thought it was a dirty place where people suffered from poverty, no education, and bad governments. But now I see it's just as good as we are. I respect their citizens, because they have to work hard for a living. Sometimes if you work hard for something, you get more out of it than if you were handed it on a silver platter."

Thanks to charitable grants, seven students from Elaine High were able to attend a Global Realities and Youth Leadership Challenge workshop in Taos, New Mexico. Their reactions were similar. Many of them had never been out of Elaine. For teenagers who had never seen an escalator, the airplane flight itself was quite an experience.

Another surprise for the workshop participants was the amount of knowledge other students had. Elaine's students came home demanding to learn more, and asked McCray to give them a special class to help them with college entrance exams, so they could get into good schools.

An additional benefit of the workshop, they reported, was the realization that not all white people are prejudiced. "The whites in New Mexico seemed to go out of their way to be nice," said one student. "In Elaine, there is a lot of prejudice. In Taos, we roomed with white kids from Iowa and New Mexico. They obviously aren't prejudiced against black people, because they treated us so friendly."

Since McCray's and Larry's principal objective was to teach that there can be more to life than picking cotton, one long-term measure of the program's success is the ability of these students to prepare for a good job. McCray would like some to return to Elaine to set an example for others. Graduates from 1989 and beyond are the ones to really test the program—they will have been in global studies for three years. Their collegiate goals have spanned a variety of different fields, including business, teaching, medicine, journalism, law, and veterinary medicine. Thus far, we know that after college, many who have graduated do plan to return to Elaine with their professional skills, while others express a desire to get away from their home town.

DISTURBING THE PEACE

With the program a popular success, both the principal and the superintendent have praised McCray and Larry. But Webster, the principal, admits he was not enthusiastic at first. "I didn't know what to expect," he said. "Miss McCray just used her imagination and creativity and came up with a really good program. It has caught the eye of the community, and has gotten good press coverage. Miss Billie is known in-state and out."

"The club has received a lot of recognition, and a number of kids have gotten to see other places and make friends outside the state," added superintendent Parker. "The community pays tribute for what they all have done. It has brought the kids closer together and raised their education level."

McCray selflessly gives much of the credit for the club's success to GIG's first president, Stephen Hall. McCray tells how the club planned, with leftover funds, to take a pizza trip to a nearby town. Hall managed to convince the administration to allow the club to use the school van, then talked the janitor into driving the group into town. Hall was an academic student, and his partner, Ronald Hall (no relation), was a popular football player. Together, they made a perfect leadership team.

The global studies class' chief sources of information and materials have been George Otero, and the Center for Teaching International Relations at the University of Denver. McCray adds that she uses everything she can get her hands on from workshops, as well as local resources— namely, "Anyone from here who has ever gone places."

A new teacher had been to Korea, and gave a presentation; the new Spanish teacher shared the year he spent in Spain; a student's visiting uncle who had been to Nigeria was asked to speak; and anyone who had traveled with the military was invited. A black man from the area told how he went to California. When he came back with his

Afro hairstyle and heels, according to him "He stuck out like a sore thumb." He contrasted this to his introduction to California when people there said, "He's obviously from the country!"

But not all of Elaine has embraced the program with open arms. The administration has received complaints from both black and white parents. This wasn't surprising to many, for in a town that had overcome a painful history of slavery few were anxious to see the status quo disrupted. Elaine has no obvious drug problems, no violence in the school hallways, a relatively low dropout rate (eight percent), obedient farm workers who work seasonally and don't have running water for their homes. It's hard to find someone who doesn't attend church regularly.

"Both blacks and whites here are very conservative," said a black resident. "They're perfectly content to stay in the same old rut. This is a farming area, and cheap labor is needed. As long as they can keep us uneducated and unskilled, they've got it made. Only the ones that get out and then come back will ever try to do anything about it."

Many sad stories can be told of those who didn't realize this in time. Lee Hall, the popular football player who organized the boycott on King's birthday, is one such case. During one class Hall was not paying attention, so McCray sent him to the principal's office. Later, she overheard the principal saying that he was not mad at Lee and was sure that she wasn't either. McCray stepped into the office and said, "Yes I am mad at you, Lee. You can't play football at Arkansas University with this attitude—you need to get something into your head."

Six months after Hall graduated from Elaine, he told McCray that he should have heeded her words. He could make the football team at the university, he told her, but not the classes. He now works for a Tennessee sanitation department.

A brighter indication of the future may be seen in the reaction of a local black farmer on hearing McCray speak to a reporter. The man had been idly listening, and suddenly broke in. "Miss Billie, I had no idea you cared so much about these kids," he said. "I thought you were only involved because of the publicity. You really do care about what happens to them. These kids need to get out and see for themselves. How about if I drive a group of kids to New Mexico next time?"

The program's success shows how much can be done with minimal material resources. Inspiring teachers like Billie McCray and Shirley Larry who use their imaginations and creativity can produce wonders. As Stephen Hall's father, the reverend Freddy Hall, put it, the way these two teachers are "hanging in and doing right" will eventually infect the whole community. With any luck, Elaine will never be the same.

CHAPTER EIGHT

McCLUER NORTH HIGH SCHOOL

Dennis Lubeck and Terry Reger

Building an international program at McCluer North High School in suburban St.Louis was a little easier for the International Education Consortium (IEC) than it was at other schools. McCluer North had the distinct advantage of beginning its history in 1971 with a principal and a faculty who, for the most part, volunteered to work at the school. McCluer North was designed to be a model operating school with shared decision-making, an out-of-school learning program, and a teacher/advisor program. The school was one of St. Louis-based IEC's original nine area schools, chosen in 1984—the same year McCluer North was the only Missouri high school to receive the U.S. Department of Education Excellence in Education award.

THE DISTRICT

McCluer North is part of the Ferguson-Florissant School District, an integrated public school system in northwest St. Louis County, adjacent to Lambert St.Louis International Airport. The district is the fourth largest of 23 suburban county districts and serves eleven cities. Students primarily come from low- and middle-income homes, although there are pockets of affluent families.

In 1975, a federal court order merged the district with two adjacent towns, Berkeley and Kinloch. Kinloch is one

of the ten poorest municipalities in the USA. Most of the
Kinloch students were assigned to McCluer North. As a
result, the student body is now 30 percent black, two percent
Asian and Hispanic, and 68 percent white.

McCluer North is one of three high schools in the
district, which also includes three middle, 15 elementary,
and one alternative school. The combined enrollment of the
district is 11,320; the annual per pupil expenditure is about
$4,822, above the average for the rest of the county.

The Ferguson-Florissant School District has a reputation
for innovation. Its early education programs—Parents as
First Teachers, Saturday School, and Child Development
programs, which provide a variety of learning activities,
home visits by teachers, and diagnostic tests for
preschoolers—have won national recognition. Environmental studies are offered through the Little Creek Wildlife
Area; at a 97-acre wildlife refuge, students are exposed to
global environmental issues and receive a practical, hands-
on nature study that is integrated with the science and social
studies curricula. PROBE is a program designed to
challenge gifted students, and the district also offers a drug
program for student suspended from school for drug or
alcohol violations.

In keeping with the recommendations made on teaching
in recent national reports, the district has been working to
give teachers more responsibility for curriculum, in-service
and management decisions. Teachers make up most of the
membership of the K-12 curriculum committee, which
reviews curriculum and examines school-wide programs.
Teachers are given opportunities for leadership through an
administrative intern program, a mini-grant program, and a
teacher-directed staff development program.

THE SCHOOL

The McCluer North staff, which is made up of an equal
number of men and women, has an impressive resume:

several faculty members serve as consultants and instructors at local universities; many have received fellowships and study project grants, and several have had articles published in professional education journals. Fifty-four percent have been at the school since 1973, and more than half have traveled to a foreign country.

McCluer North's spacious library, cafeteria, and advisement center help create a climate of camaraderie and openness within the school.

To further address the needs of the students, McCluer North provides coursework for high school students of varying abilities and interests. Academically motivated students can receive credit for college and honors courses. The school also provides a team-taught Core 9 program for "at-risk" 9th graders, and an interdisciplinary English and social studies course. The Community outreach program allows students to work as aides in an elementary school, day care center, a school for the handicapped, or in a hospital setting. This program was recently cited as one of the top ten in the nation by a University of Wisconsin study.

The most effective way for McCluer North teachers to monitor student development is the Advisory Program, which integrates academic and personal life. Every staff member accepts responsibility for the learning program and personal growth of 15 to 20 students during their high school career. The advisor meets weekly with his or her advisees in a group setting, and then for an additional two hours each month.

Eighty-five percent of McCluer North's students participate in the school's 40 extracurricular activities, ranging from a Computer Club to the Black Heritage Committee. There is also a complete athletic program. This balance of academic and extracurricular activities has led to 25-30 percent of the students receiving college scholarships. Follow-up surveys show that nearly half of the respondents enroll in a four-year college or university, 17 percent enroll in a community college, ten percent enroll in vocational training, two percent enlist in the military and 17 percent find full-time employment right after high school.

Bill Hampton, who served as principal from 1971 to 1986, like his successor Larry Kreyling, involves teachers in decision making through the Program Improvement Committee (PIC), which meets weekly to discuss problems and set goals. The PIC includes department chairs, a counselor, and several other teachers chosen by the principal. Hampton and then-superintendent of schools Dan Keck viewed international studies as a tool for investing in teachers and for increasing interdisciplinary cooperation. They saw global studies as a way to counter the fragmentation of knowledge in the state-mandated curriculum.

THE OUTSIDE AGENCY

That's where the International Education Consortium (IEC) stepped in.

The IEC is a cooperative effort by university, corporate and community organizations to help secondary schools increase students' knowledge of world affairs.

The IEC's goal is to widen the perspective of teachers, and eventually their students, by providing the most up-to-date information, skills, and techniques available from the local community of universities, multinational corporations, and cultural resources. The result is energized, motivated, and committed teachers in many disciplines who become instructional leaders in their classroom, their school, and their district.

The governing structure of the IEC provides the resources to design the challenging programs offered to the school community. The policy board includes liberal arts deans from local universities, representatives from multinational corporations, individuals from the St. Louis chapters of the World Affairs Council and the United Nations Association, and teachers and central office administrators from local school districts. The IEC also works with an advisory panel made up of the chancellors of major universities, the directors of leading local cultural institutions, executives from multinational coporations, and representatives of the leading local community organizations.

HISTORY AND STRATEGY

With monetary support from the Danforth, James S. McDonnell and Rockefeller Foundations, the IEC began work in the summer of 1984 with multidisciplinary teams of five to ten teachers from each of nine high schools. New schools have been added each year and the consortium currently works with 11 city schools, 2 inner-suburban schools, 13 suburban schools, and 1 rural school in the greater St.Louis metropolitan area.

The IEC staff serves as a bridge between schools and community resources, using multiple strategies to promote the humanities, social sciences, the arts, and science through the intellectual framework of international education. Strategies include (1) identifying interdisciplinary teams of lead teachers from participating schools who receive consultant services and participate in special programming, (2) offering workshops featuring content in specific disciplines to teachers throughout the St.Louis area, (3) organizing seminars and evening programs with multinational corporations and local universities, (4) establishing a resource center for the use of individual teachers, (5) publishing a newsletter, and (6) designing opportunities to educate administrators about the importance of the humanities and international education.

The IEC works primarily with teams of teachers who are designated as instructional leaders by their principals. As a group, the teachers attend a yearly week-long summer institute and at least two one-day workshops during the year; these all have multidisciplinary formats and content. A goal is to expose the teachers to knowledge and forms of expression from outside their teaching disciplines. In the summer of 1988, an audience of teachers of literature, history, science, and foreign languages attended an institute on Islam which included presentations on history, current politics, contemporary writers, and the impact of religion on politics.

IEC staff members meet with school teams throughout the year to help teachers integrate content and methods from workshops into individual classrooms and the curriculum, and to design plans to expose teachers and administrators in each school to international education. With administrative backing, team activities are translated into programs for wider audiences including (a) countless inservice presentations featuring introductory or more specific discipline-related content; (b) "International Weeks," involving the whole school and sometimes the community; (c) curriculum projects such as those resulting in many non-Western writers being used across the language arts curriculum; (d) the creation of new courses in the humanities and comparative political systems; and (e) expansion of traditional Western civilization courses to include non-Western history.

The programs IEC offered McCluer North staff members included a seminar for language arts and Spanish teachers on the boom in Latin American literature; a dinner discussion for educators with Pacific Rim representatives of multinational corporations; a day-long workshop for physics teachers on the international implications of superconductivity; a workshop for foreign language teachers on how to integrate international business with the teaching of a foreign language; a week-long summer institute on Latin America and Africa; one-day institutes for social studies teachers on the Israeli-Palestinian conflict; and a six-week curriculum project in India for 15 teachers funded by the U.S. Department of Education's Fulbright Office.

McCLUER NORTH'S FIRST IEC FELLOWS

When McCluer North was first invited to be a member of the IEC in 1984, principal Hampton was required to choose a team of five teachers. He didn't simply go to the faculty to ask for volunteers; instead, he recruited five faculty leaders: Terry Reger, who had a reputation for imaginative teaching; Ted Lotz, who had the ability to translate other cultures to the U.S. culture; Joan Avioli, admired by the faculty for her worldliness and intellect; Chuck Westover, a maverick science teacher who believed that science should be taken out of the laboratory and applied to technology and environmental issues, particularly in the Third World; and Joyce Evans, the librarian, known for her close relationship with the faculty.

The group's first task was to attend a week-long summer institute and two one-day workshops to learn more about international issues. They also attended lectures and workshops on international issues given by local universities, the United Nations Association and the World Affairs Council.

With help from the IEC, the team became better informed on a variety of topics and issues. Equally important, they were exposed to an array of professors in the fields of art, music, history, political science, literature, science, and medicine—all of which underlined for them the interdisciplinary nature of international studies.

The Fellows used their acquired knowledge and IEC linkages to share their experiences with their colleagues. Principal Hampton's backing was crucial in giving them early opportunities to explain the IEC at department and faculty meetings, and he supported the team's inservice day devoted to a series of seminars on China, the Soviet Union, and international business. Hampton also adopted international education as one of the five major goals of the school.

The IEC also provided McCluer North with a $2,000 materials grant to purchase international reference materials for the school. The Fellows, wanting to cover every discipline in the school, spent the funds on books, magazines, graphics, and slides. The materials were placed in the library for use by all the faculty.

During the spring of 1985, Hampton and the teachers broadened the school's traditional "Foreign Festival," a one-day program sponsored by the foreign language department, into a five-day International Week. Every discipline got involved, and so did the community. The social studies department put student projects and other displays in the instructional materials center. Chuck Westover, a science teacher, created computer lessons on identifying Third World countries. But the math department stole the show by organizing the simulated conversion of dollars into foreign currency such as yen, franc, peso, and lira in order to purchase food and attend cultural performances during the International Week. International foods were prepared by both the home economics and foreign language departments.

Activities during the week were dominated by global topics. Students and parents attened seminars on international issues, from the Nicaraguan Revolution to international trade. The Week included an evening of food and culture for the entire community served by the Ferguson-Florissant School District. The last day of the International Week was an international film festival organized by the English Department.

MORE TEACHERS GET INVOLVED

During the next three years, the team continued to develop new ideas for influencing the faculty and the school district. Initiated by Ted Lotz, they developed a Forum Series on international issues for parents, students, and faculty members. The series began with "Children of War," which focused on the effects of war on children. Other programs included German education, and a demonstration by a performing troupe from Tibet. Prior to each forum, teachers were given information to share with their students.

As a result of their work with IEC, several McCluer North teachers won fellowships and grants. Carl Yochum, an art teacher, was awarded a trip to India with his student Joel Mangrum in a nationwide competition sponsored by the Asia Society of New York. Ellen Bowles, a foreign language teacher, won a scholarship to attend a summer institute on international business sponsored by the St. Louis University School of International Business. Jane Helbig, a physical education teacher and photographer, joined Terry Reger as a Fulbright Fellow when the IEC received a grant to take 15 teachers to India for 6 weeks.

A team-taught humanities course was created by Carl Yochum, Joan Avioli, and Larry Marsh, a social studies teacher and music critic for the *St.Louis Post-Dispatch*. The program was funded by a district mini-grant which gave each teacher an extra planning period to design the course and a grant from the IEC to purchase audiovisual materials. The content of the course is truly international. Students are exposed to a Western and a non-Western perspective of the visual arts, music, and literature. The course covers Indian Moghul miniature paintings, the stories and music which they depict and the cultural values which they reveal. Classic Chinese poetry, works such as *One Hundred Years of Solitude*, a novel by Gabriel Garcia Marquez, German and Russian symphonic music and ancient Persian epics are just some of the resources used in the course.

IEC participation has encouraged McCluer North faculty to think in international terms. English courses now include more novels, plays, short stories and poetry by African, Latin American, and Asian authors. Librarian Marsha Pfingston has noted a change in the focus of issues chosen for student projects. In the past four years, Pfingston has purchased more books, materials, and newspapers on global issues, in response to increasing requests by both teachers and students, than she did in the past.

In the social studies department, Joe Naumann compiled a unit on world religions to be used by 6th and 11th grade teachers. Terry Reger is working on "Living on the Edge," and "Passages to India," two audio curriculum projects developed by teachers with the assistance of Julian Crandall Hallick, a radio journalist whose reports are heard on National Public Radio, and Marilyn Turkovich, a prominent American curriculum writer on Asia. The work is to be published by the Asia Society.

Reger continued her commitment to international studies when she was promoted, in 1988, to become social studies coordinator for the Ferguson-Florissant School District. Prior to her new job, she helped develop a year-long world history course with other social studies teachers in the district.

NEXT STEP: DISSEMINATION

While the McCluer North team has influenced the curriculum and spirit of their school, as well as the district's requirements in social studies, their impact on other schools in the district is in its initial stages. Many administrators and teachers are only now becoming aware of the significance of international education. Arnold Potts, Acting Superintendent of Curriculum, and John Wright, Assistant Superintendent of Personnel, are encouraging other administrators and teachers to become more involved in international studies. The district placed the following statement in its strategic plan: "*A complete education is impossible without an understanding of and respect for our own and other cultures.*"

There are many other promising examples of the district's commitment to the necessary staff and curriculum development for the growth of teachers in this area. The International Culture Center will be an ongoing project which will provide resources for teachers, maintain current information and samples for curriculum planning and classroom use, connect teachers to people in the community with international expertise, and communicate international education opportunities for teachers. International festivals were organized for all three high schools in the district in 1989, and the three middle schools in 1990.

The Springboard to Learning Program, a multicultural "hands-on" enrichment program which brings specialists from all over the world into classrooms, was planned for each middle school during 1989-90. Culture kits, assembled by educators who have visited foreign countries, have been developed. One-day seminars on select world issues—e.g., Greenhouse Effect, World Debt and the Changing Role of Women—were held in 1989.

WHAT HAS BEEN LEARNED

Although the future expansion of international education in the Ferguson-Florissant School District is dependent on the attitude of an ever changing new crop of teachers and administrators, several lessons have been learned based on McCluer North's experiences thus far:

1. Curriculum reform depends on a partnership between teachers and administrators;

2. Site-based management is crucial for influencing the faculty;

3. An independent agency with community linkages is often better equipped than a school district to introduce teachers to the newest information about international issues;

4. Teachers' professional lives are generally isolated from sources of intellectual renewal and development;

5. Inservice and curriculum development too often offers pedagogy without considering the need for further study;

6. International studies maintains high academic standards, while preparing students for the future;

7. International studies is interdisciplinary by definition;

8. University professors are generally interested in assisting teachers;

9. Organizations like IEC raise the self-esteem of teachers and given fresh energy to schools.

The IEC's experience confirms the view of those who speak for the necessary relationship between the involvement of teachers in curriculum decision-making, self-respect and genuine intellectual growth. When teachers leave their isolation and gain a perspective on the content of their discipline and the relationship of that discipline to others, they no longer have to defer to the whims of the "experts," whether they are supervisors or textbook publishers. More confident, better educated teachers can only benefit schools and students.

CHAPTER NINE

PARK VIEW K-8 SCHOOL

Ken Tye and Kathy O'Neil

Forty miles south of Los Angeles and tucked up against the Pacific coast in Orange County is the city of Huntington Beach, a sprawling suburban middle-to-upper-class community. In the center of a residential neighborhood in Huntington Beach stands Park View School, a K-8 elementary school which until recently was an integral part of the Ocean View School District. In June of 1988, the school was closed because of declining enrollment in the district; but for three years, until the school's closing, the Center for Human Interdependence (CHI) worked with the staff to bring a global focus to the existing Park View curriculum.

During the time that CHI was at Park View, the size of the school hovered between 450 and 500 students. About half of the student population lived with only one parent. Nearly three-quarters of the students were from homes in which the single parent or, in the case of two-parent homes, both parents worked. The ethnic majority of the student body was Caucasian, with approximately 23 percent of the students of Asian, black, or Hispanic backgrounds. Although the parents' involvement in daytime school activities was at times limited because of their work schedules, their attendance at special school programs, as well as their cooperation on home-school decisions and procedures, reflected solid interest and support. The physical environment of the school was extremely pleasant, demonstrating the creative abilities of both staff and students as well as the attitude that this was a "home away from home" and, as such, it should be—and was— comfortable and welcoming. The building itself was a modern, one-level unit with a partially open, flexible floor plan. Students were grouped in kindergarten, primary, intermediate, and 7th-8th grade pods which were arranged in an imperfect square around a central outdoor patio. Most of the classrooms, particularly the ones in the primary and intermediate areas, had a feeling of openness; they often had only three walls, allowing the classrooms to be open to a common space where students and teachers could move about, yet the carpeted floors allowed this to happen quietly. Some classrooms had movable dividers for creating flexible space where groups within pods could be convened for special activities. The Library Learning Center, a frequently-used resource for teachers and students alike, was centrally located in an attractive, open, and much-traveled area with easy access from all classrooms.

Grades K-6 were self-contained, whereas grades 7 and 8 had departmentalized programs. Emphasis was on developing basic skills at all levels, but the junior high program had additional quiet reading, study skills, and exploratory programs. Computer-assisted instruction was endorsed to varying degrees at all grade levels and several programs existed for handicapped children or students with other special needs. Except for advanced reading and algebra programs in the 7th and 8th grades and a gifted and talented (GATE) program operating in grades 4-8, classes were heterogeneously grouped with students of all ability levels.

SOMEONE SPECIAL

None of the above characteristics make Park View School stand out particularly from most California elementary schools in similar socioeconomic environments. Yet, soon after the CHI project was initiated at the school, it became apparent that Park View was, in fact, special, at least in terms of global education. The project was allowed entree into the school and the classrooms, and experienced firsthand the interactions among teachers as well as between teachers and students. Park View's uniqueness, it was soon realized, stemmed from two sources: the leadership and support of the school's principal, Janet Reece; and the superior calibre of the Park View teachers and their openness to the idea of developing global awareness.

Initial insights into Janet Reece's role as a key player in creating a global focus at Park View came in the fall of CHI's first year: 1985. Prior to meeting with the teachers for the first time, the CHI staff met with Reece to introduce the project to her. She responded enthusiastically, sharing that she saw the project giving refreshing perspectives and opportunities to teachers. She felt that giving teachers exposure to new ideas through workshops as well as providing them with release time, opportunities to develop new curriculum, and access to the CHI library resources would enhance the work that the teachers were already doing, and would energize them. The idea of letting each teacher decide the extent and direction of his or her own involvement with the project was also very well accepted by Reece, who knew that the imposition of too many mandated programs and requirements often leads to teacher burnout and low staff morale. The CHI project, in giving the teachers choice about their participation, was, in her view, not a threat to the teachers' enthusiasm for teaching but, instead, a potential source of professional renewal for them. Throughout the three years of CHI involvement at Park View, high priorities for Reece included concern for the welfare of her teachers, encouragement of them to be decision-makers at the school level, and recognition of them as experts in their fields. It is no wonder that Reece was loved by her staff and considered by them to be a top-notch principal; and that teacher morale at Park View was excellent.

Reece's words of support for CHI a month later at the first Park View faculty presentation were important in getting the project off to a good start. The teachers heard her emphasize that this project offered opportunity for their professional growth, was non-imposing, and could augment the curriculum of those teachers who chose to become involved. A week later, Reece confirmed what had been sensed on the day of that first presentation: the initial contact had produced a very positive response from the teachers.

WAITING FOR THE HOOK

Yet, simultaneously with the apparent philosophical acceptance of the project, the teachers expressed a concern that would take time to overcome: "Would there be any hooks? Any requirements that would have to be fulfilled? Any extra work that would later be piled onto an already heavy work load?" The answer to them, of course, was no. But even with Reece's clear backing of the program, teachers were still not fully convinced that CHI was there to do what it said it would do: offer global awareness resources for teachers and ask nothing in return. Reece, who later proved to be right, gave assurance that in time the teachers' doubts would dissipate. So the project forged ahead, with Janet at its side, hoping to enthuse and stimulate an initial group of Park View teachers to think about infusing this thing called a "global perspective" into their existing curriculum.

The project at Park View differed from many others described in this volume in that there was not an identifiable group of teachers who started with an avowed interest in global education. Everyone at Park View began with about the same level of commitment and knowledge.

THREE PRODUCTIVE YEARS

During the first year of the project, there were some teachers who were more active than others, to be sure, but there were no "stars." Over half of the 25 faculty members were involved in one way or another during that first year, 1985-86. Sixty-three items were checked out of the CHI library (books, slide sets, films, activity packages or kits, puzzles, games), and ten teachers attended CHI workshops on such topics as cross-cultural awareness, global economics, environmental issues, and folklore/folk art. CHI staff members visited the school six times during the year for meetings with the principal, groups of teachers, and individual teachers. While the initial two meetings of teachers focused upon global "themes" (e.g., world hunger, endangered species, nuclear arms/world peace, energy), no one theme emerged for the entire school. Instead, individual teachers worked to follow their own interests and/or to bring a global perspective to what they were already doing. In the final month of that first year, nine upper elementary and junior high level classes put on an international day. Various presentations were made, and food, clothing, and dances were sampled and demonstrated. Parents were invited, and many even assisted.

At the end of the year, CHI staff met with Janet Reece and Paul Mercier, Assistant Superintendent of Instruction for the Ocean View School District, and reported to them about the activities at Park View during the first year. Principal Reece was very positive about everything that had happened. Tentative plans were made for the second year, including the allocation of release days for teachers to attend inservice activities. This was done despite impending major cuts in the district and school budgets.

During year 2, 19 of the 25 faculty members at Park View participated in the project. Regular activities included checking out curriculum materials from the CHI library, visits of CHI staff to the school, and attendance at CHI workshops by some Park View faculty members. The workshops during year two included (1) working with immigrant and refugee children [Orange County is a "gateway" community for immigrants and refugees], (2) folk dance, and (3) dealing with controversial issues in the classroom. This last workshop featured Steve Lamy, a noted global educator from the University of Southern California. In addition, 50 7th graders, evenly divided between boys and girls, attended an International Sports Day at Chapman College, featuring cooperative games from around the world. Linda Hayward, a P.E. teacher at Park View, was a member of the network-wide committee which planned the Sports Day.

Four mini-grants totalling $3,600 were given by CHI to Park View teachers during the 1986-87 year. With this money, two teachers developed a five-week study of environmental interdependence for grades 4, 5, and 7; two other teachers developed a Spanish language and culture course for grades 6-8; one teacher developed an ethnic foods unit for grade 7; and two teachers developed a study of ethnic, cultural, and religious diversity in Orange County for grades 7-8.

There was also a special "multicultural awareness" presentation made to the faculty in the spring of '87 by George Otero of Las Palomas de Taos Education Center. It was interesting that principals from two other schools in the district, and two district administrators, attended this presentation.

The level of participation at Park View remained at about 80 percent during the third (and, as it turned out, the final) year of the project at the school. As stated earlier, it was closed at the end of the 1987-88 year because of declining enrollments in the district.

As during the two previous years, at Park View several dozen items were checked out from the CHI library and CHI staff members continued to visit the school regularly. Another 50 7th graders participated in the 2nd annual

International Sports Day, and teachers from Park View continued to attend CHI theme workshops.

Four more mini-grants were awarded to Park View teachers during 1987-88. They totalled $2,300 and were used for (1) a grades 1-2 study of folk literature, poetry, and music around the world; (2) a collection of library books dealing with cultural commonalities among families of the world for grades 7-8; (3) an endangered species unit for the middle grades developed by a 6th grade teacher and a teacher of learning handicapped students; and (4) a special global education section in the library developed by the librarian.

There were two CHI-sponsored special presentations during the year. In November, Dr. David Cohen from Australia spoke to some 120 upper elementary and junior high students about life in his country. In December, George Otero returned, to address multicultural issues with the staff. They were joined by the staffs of the two schools of the principals who had heard him speak the previous spring.

During 1987-88, one Park View teacher participated in CHI's "Your Community and the World" project, then in its second year. This activity, in which students from several CHI network schools identified and tracked the many connections between their own community and the rest of the world, at Park View formed part of an all-school "Our Earth" display which included interdisciplinary activities at all grade levels.

LEARNING FROM THE EXPERIENCE

One of the distinguishing features of the CHI project was that it was, in fact, designed as a research study. At Park View, for example, teachers were frequently interviewed informally, and those interviews were written up. Classroom visits were likewise written up. At the end of the 1987-88 year, all of the teachers, the principal, and the Assistant Superintendent were interviewed more formally. Some of the results of this data-gathering effort are interesting.

In classroom visits at Park View, teachers were seen making use of much of the content already discussed in this chapter. Students were learning about endangered species and other environmental issues. There was much focus on cross-cultural similarities and differences. Students were learning about such concepts as location, time, space, community, and conflict. The standard curriculum was being infused with a global perspective, and some new "global" curriculum was being introduced. There was much integration of subject matter—e.g., social studies and science with language arts, the fine arts, and the practical arts.

In terms of instruction, there was a great deal of cooperative group work and other forms of active learning such as interviewing, field trips, panel presentations, and construction. There was also evidence of thoughtful questioning by teachers. There was very little of the "teacher talks-students read the book-students answer the questions" pedagogy which is so deadly and, unfortunately, characteristic of too many of America's classrooms.

The critical point is that at Park View, global education served as an organizing theme which allowed teachers to design and implement classroom units that utilized sound principles of curriculum and instruction. CHI did not specifically focus on such principles, and there was a highly competent group of teachers at this school. Global educators, however, should take note that questions of how to organize for and carry out instruction (pedagogy) are as important as what should be taught (content), particularly if the question one wants to answer is, "What does it take to bring a global perspective to the curriculum of a school?"

Teacher interviews confirmed the importance of the principal to the globalization of the Park View curriculum. Teachers perceived Janet Reece as supportive and facilitating. She was seen as having the ability to encourage without pressuring, to match faculty with inservice opportunities, to keep people informed, and to be sensitive to the many demands placed upon their time.

The interviews also confirmed the importance to the change process of the presence of an outside agency such as

CHI. However, in the beginning, teachers were "waiting for the hook." That is, they could not believe that there would not be reports to write, tests to administer, or some type of extraordinary requirement. Once it was seen that CHI would not be making demands, teachers frequently took advantage of what was offered. When asked, at the end, whether CHI should have perhaps been more assertive, several interviewees said that would not have worked; people would have resisted.

Perhaps the biggest barriers to the globalization of the curriculum at Park View was the fact that there were so many competing demands on teachers' time. There was district-wide adoption of new math, science, and reading curricula, the latter being a new literature-based program which was a major change. There was a mandated child abuse prevention program, an emphasis upon testing and assuring high test scores, and there were all of the regular pressures of teaching. Whenever possible, as with the literature program, CHI worked to make a global perspective fit in with other concerns. However, there is no doubt that competing demands on teacher time is a major barrier to bringing a global perspective to the curriculum of a school.

Interviews with the assistant superintendent and principal were revealing, also. Assistant Superintendent Paul Mercier said that the district had had some concern initially because there were some conservative elements in the community whom they feared might object to global education. They had faith in both the principal and in CHI leadership, however, and decided to proceed. As it turned out, there were no problems and, in fact, the community was supportive. The International Sports Day, for example, was seen as good public relations. Other initial concerns were financial, and just what the district might get out of the CHI project. Mercier indicated real support for the more or less non-directive strategy adopted by CHI, thought the project had been successful, and estimated that a school curriculum could be globalized using a similar strategy over a longer period of time. He acknowledged the key role played by the principal.

Principal Reece reflected that her initial concern had to do with the amount of work that might be imposed upon teachers. By the end of three years, she was quite pleased with what had happened. She felt that almost everyone at the school had been touched by CHI and that the infusion of a global perspective was pervasive in classes at the school. She felt that workshops, site visits, and the other strategies already discussed had been helpful. She pointed to the CHI quarterly newsletters as being of value, also. However, Reece indicated that she would have liked to have had more contact with the other network principals during the course of the project.

CONCLUDING THOUGHTS

In some ways, Park View was a unique school. Ocean View School District has a history of innovative programs. Administrators there understand the change process, and support the notion of the single school as the unit upon which improvement efforts should be focused. Also, the principal had a personal background which included living, traveling, and studying overseas; being a social studies teacher; and being raised in a family which was alert to global issues. Equally important, she understood what it takes to make a school run. The faculty was experienced and, yet, eager to continue to grow. They were cosmopolitan; they were professionals.

There is a paucity of research in the field of global education, particularly research on what it takes to change schools to ones that have a global perspective. There is, however, much good research on educational change, in general. What we need now are studies of what actually happens when faculties attempt to "bring a global perspective" to their curriculum.

It is too bad that Park View had to be closed because of declining enrollments, for it was becoming a school with a global perspective. Fortunately, that "becoming" was documented, and other educators have the opportunity to learn from it.

CHAPTER TEN

MIAMI HIGH SCHOOL

Toni Fuss-Kirkwood

Within the heart of Miami's "Little Havana" lies Miami Senior High School. The student body reflects the ethnic composition of the neighborhood: 90 percent of the 2,500 students are Hispanic, and 8 percent are black.

Miami High is part of the Dade County Public School District, the fourth largest in the nation. With 260,000 students, the district employs 15,000 teachers and has an annual operating budget of $1.24 billion. Elementary schools numbering 178 feed into 48 middle-junior high schools and 25 senior high schools.

Established in 1906, Miami High is the county's oldest high school. The community takes pride in the school's Norman-Sicilian architecture, adapted from the Romanesque. Many of Miami High's original building materials were imported from Spain and Portugal. Luscious courtyards, surrounding gurgling fountains, invite the passers-by.

CHOOSING A GLOBAL FOCUS SCHOOL-WIDE

But what makes Miami High special is more than just its cosmetic appearance. For the 1985-86 and 1986-87 school years, the school made global education the major focus of its Quality Instruction Incentive Program (QUIIP), the Dade County version of the Florida State Merit School Program.

QUIIP, which was agreed upon by the school board and the United Teachers of Dade County, established different levels of meritorious school and employee awards as well as commensurate pay bonuses.

To participate in QUIIP, schools must fulfill four requirements: submit plans to improve Stanford Achievement Test scores; increase student attendance; enroll the majority of students in physical fitness programs; and develop a proposal to improve specific standards of excellence. For the latter, Miami High chose to emphasize a global perspective throughout its multidisciplined curriculum.

The strategies selected to implement a global approach began with a September meeting to "set the mood." The elected faculty council presented the plan to all the teachers. Principal Diego Garcia, Jr. explained the need for global education, asking teachers to "think globally and act locally."

The department chairs then met to coordinate specific strategies for their subject areas. They, in turn, met with their department members to work out the specifics. This democratic procedure allowed teachers to fully participate in the decision-making process.

K-12/UNIVERSITY LINKAGES

The global facilitators, who were classroom teachers acting as liaisons between the schools and Florida International University's College of Education Global Awareness Program, provided program support throughout the year—both to individual educators and at group meetings.

The facilitators are experienced classroom teachers who are placed on special assignment to the University by the school district. New global teachers with leadership skills are systematically identified and included in the training of new groups of teachers. This process of master teachers teaching other teachers enables the program to have widespread impact.

The leadership training and program development format is designed around these phases:

> **Conceptualization:** Teachers and administrators are introduced to the conceptual framework for a global perspective by Global Awareness Program facilitators.

> **Inventory:** Assisted by the facilitators, building personnel survey their school's program, needs, and resources; and identify potential opportunities for infusing a global perspective into the curriculum.

> **Design:** Teachers and administrators, assisted by the Global Awareness Program staff, design a program for the infusion of global education that is tailored to the individual school and feeder pattern.

> **Implementation:** Clinical assistance, including demonstration instruction, is provided by the Global Awareness Program staff. Administrators are encouraged to include global education objectives at the building, area, and district levels. Methods and materials workshops and content seminars are offered by the Florida International University faculty.

> **Network:** Opportunities are provided for teachers and administrators to share their ideas with others, through professional organization conferences and journals. A newsletter and an achievement award program sponsored by the Global Awareness Program assist in this process.

> **Assessment:** Pre and post assessments of teacher and student knowledge and attitudes are compared. The data are used as part of the knowledge base needed for program maintenance and revision.

A WORKABLE DEFINITION

The Dade County global education program, of which Miami High is a part, is guided by use of the Robert Hanvey definition of global education. It serves as a basis for the training of teachers.(1) It fits well, because teachers in Florida are bound by state level curriculum frameworks and district curriculum objectives. Thus, in Dade County, as in many places around the country, global education is probably best approached through an "infusion" strategy rather than through the establishment of separate courses. The Hanvey model supports such a strategy.

In the process of globalizing the curriculum, the Dade County program has fostered the following kinds of classroom activities:

1. **Perspective Consciousness.** Teachers have been encouraged to have students compare and contrast such things as the roles of family members, treatment of the elderly, child-rearing, eating habits, and courtship patterns across cultures. In examining social customs and values, students gain insights into various perspectives and begin to see that their views are not the only ones in the world.

2. **State of the Planet Awareness.** Teachers are taught to have students examine current events, use maps to locate places in the world where events occur, and link current events to historical patterns and happenings. Most important, they are taught to have students speculate about the culture. "What if...becomes an important springboard.

3. **Cross-Cultural Awareness.** With 136 nations represented by the student body of Dade County schools, teachers are taught to utilize local community resources, and to view students and their families as resource as well. Further, they are encouraged to use cross-cultural simulations, pen pals and a variety of other active learning procedures.

4. **Knowledge of Global Dynamics.** This is perhaps the most critical dimension of the Hanvey framework. Teachers need to teach students to understand the systemic and interdependent nature of events and issues. They need to have students continually look for unintended consequences of actions, and they need to help students develop understanding of how cultural, ecological, economic, political, and technological systems work and compare.

5. **Awareness of Human Choices.** In Dade County, the notion that one should "think globally and act locally" is emphasized. This leads to such class projects as adopting a nursing home; conducting an anti-litter, aluminum can, or paper drive campaign; having a sister school in a Third World country; studying the plight of immigrant groups in the community;or examining the various aspects of a local problem such as home-lessness and/or hunger.

THE MIAMI HIGH PROGRAM

At Miami High School, global perspectives permeated all subjects of the curriculum, with social studies serving as the lead department because of its interdisciplinary nature. In U.S. and world history classes, historical events and their international repercussions were studied. For example, the immigration wave at the end of the 19th century was compared with today's immigration, with special focus on how the phenomenon affected the United States in general and Miami in particular.

Economics classes studied the interdependence of nations in trade and communication and debated the issues arising from these interactions, with an eye toward their impact on south Florida. Students were shown how the current practice of apartheid in South Africa parallels our own history. Government classes analyzed the written constitutions of different countries and compared civil and political rights in different nations.

Cultural studies of the nations of the Caribbean basin and Central and South America brought a better understanding and appreciation of the countries that represent major immigrant groups in south Florida. Special emphasis on geography skills became second nature with daily classroom instruction.

Other subject areas also were drawn in. Students in language arts compared world literature and the effects of foreign languages on English. In home economics and family living, students discussed international banking and its effect on south Florida; foreign influences on American eating habits; foreign architecture and its influence on Miami's buildings; and child development, courtship, and family practices in foreign countries.

Mathematics students studied the logic of the metric system. They researched the evolution of Arabic and Roman numerals, compared various devices used for measurement and weight in different parts of the world, and graphed global population changes. West Germany's declining birth rate was compared with the booming population growth of Brazil and Nigeria. Students, working in groups, proposed solutions in both instances.

Students in science studied the causes and effects of various types of pollution. They debated the pros and cons of nuclear energy, comparing and contrasting Turkey Point, Miami's nearby nuclear power plant, with the Chernobyl Plant in the USSR.

Teachers of foreign languages emphasized the cultural contributions of French, German and Spanish immigrants to America's heritage. The study of foreign newspapers and magazines reinforced language skills and brought out different points of view. Art teachers demonstrated the similar techniques for making clay pots used by different cultures around the world. Also, the styles and media of international artists and their influences on American art were analyzed. Students of industrial arts compared tools, technology and careers on a worldwide scale. They discussed professions related to foreign trade and the importance of adequate tools for higher crop yields in developing nations.

The physical education and music programs played a vital role in the global program. The varsity basketball team, featuring immigrants from Colombia, Haiti, Cuba, Nicaragua and Venezuela won both the district and the regional championships during the two years of the project. The music program consisted of tunes by foreign composers, while the marching band alternated between Latin salsa and Sousa marches.

To tie all the programs together, the social studies, foreign language and language arts teachers emphasized the differing countries represented in the student body, and their contributions to the world. Breaking down cultural barriers and promoting cooperation became the underlying goal of QUIIP.

During global education's second year at Miami High, the focus remained on the interdependence of global networks and south Florida's place in these systems. The highlight of the year was the Homecoming parade, with two bands playing international music. Twenty-one countries reflecting Miami High's cosmopolitan student population were represented in their native costumes. The "Around the World" theme summed it up.

Conceptual teaching became the primary mode of instruction. Guest speakers included representatives from the Peace Corps, the Council for International Visitors, United States Information Agency, and international students from Florida International University.

"Two points are critical for a successful global education program," said principal Garcia. "Open your school up to guest speakers. For us, they added that special touch of excitement. And include your media specialist. His or her up-to-date resources and cooperation with teachers can make a real difference."

To evaluate the program, the faculty council developed its own Global Perspective pre- and post-test for each year. This required common planning and decision-making, resulting in real faculty ownership. The improvement of faculty morale formed an important part of the overall school improvement.

Test items ranged from geography skills, world events and global issues and values, to the ability to make inferences, attitudes about other nations and people, and foreign currencies and measurements. The test results over the two-year span indicated that a majority of the students made significant gains in their ability to locate places on the world map, and exhibited a greater understanding of world events, their global ramifications, and their impact on south Florida.

The integration of a global perspective into the entire school is a strong motivator for teaching and learning. It has given Miami Senior High School a fresh direction; enthusiasm is high among students and faculty.

"The best single result of global education," said Garcia, "is the unifying effect on our students—it has been a bond that brings and holds us together."

As it is true in other areas, new ideas about global education are not always adopted by the entire faculty. But there are enough dedicated and committed teachers with leadership potential—if given the opportunity to be part of the planning and decision-making—who will carry the torch into their classrooms and make a difference on a schoolwide basis.

NOTES

1 Robert G. Hanvey. *An Attainable Global Perspective.* Denver: Center for Teaching International Relations, 1976.

CHAPTER ELEVEN

ADLAI STEVENSON HIGH SCHOOL

Jonathan Swift

The setting for the 13-year-old School of Global Education is Livonia, Michigan, a Detroit suburb which boasts the nation's highest median income of all cities its size. A "bedroom community" with no commercial center, Livonia's 100,000 residents are of predominantly European ancestry with fewer than 200 blacks. The largest occupational groups in the city are managerial and professional.

Economics aside, the Livonia Public Schools District has had problems. Staff layoffs were necessary throughout the 1980s due to declining enrollment. Total loss of students during the decade exceeded 4,000, bringing the school district population to approximately 14,000. The shrinking number of faculty positions has directly hurt the global education program, which had been staffed by the newer teachers who were more likely to be laid off.

A SCHOOL-WITHIN-A-SCHOOL

The School of Global Education is a school-within-a-school located in Livonia's 1,900-student Adali Stevenson High School. The program, which recently became a magnet, uses classrooms largely confined to one wing of the high school. The global education students go out into the larger school to use the library, gym, and pool; and for some other classes.

While the faculty of the School has changed considerably over the last ten years—losing young teachers with low seniority—there has been some stability in the recent years. The six teachers now involved in the program (Louis Blunt, George Croll, Richard Holt, Gary Kleinow, Harry Nickels and Marge Sebastian) all have master's degrees and are in their 40's. Their outlook is global, stemming partly from continued travel overseas with student groups and a considerable involvement with the Great Lakes Model United Nations.

HISTORY AND STRUCTURE OF THE PROGRAM

The School of Global Education had its start in 1976 after the Michigan Department of Education staff announced competitive grants would be available under the federal Title 4-C to support innovative global education programs.

A meeting was soon arranged between the Livonia District Curriculum Department and Stevenson High's department chairs of English, science, social studies and mathematics. It was determined that a dual-focus proposal would be submitted, for both a multi-disciplined global education program and an alternative school-within-a-school. The proposal was approved, and a grant of $54,000 was awarded.

Using the 1977-78 school year for development, the School of Global Education opened in September, 1978. The newly-formed faculty advisory committee determined a set of goals for the program, and set out to make students aware of

* world literature, languages and the arts, and how these affect national behaviors;

* community, national and international economic relationships and problems;

* decision- and judgment-making processes based on the evaluation of data;

* scientific and technological achievements and their relation to society;

* the relationship between people and natural resources, and between the goals of the United States and those of other nations;

* the nature of national and international law and the use of law in resolving conflict;

* and the history, geography, and development of the Earth.

Broader goals of the alternative school included (1) providing opportunity for individual learning by allowing more choices of study, (2) allowing an interdisciplinary focus on international issues, and (3) increasing flexibility in scheduling and mobility in using community resources. Other goals included fostering closer relationships among students, parents, and teachers; and providing an opportunity for students of different ethnic and academic backgrounds and aptitudes to work and learn together.

In the program's first three years, a year-long syllabus of instruction was developed for each discipline. The curriculum soon included three years each of English, Spanish, social studies, science and mathematics.

English and social studies followed a loose chronological approach ranging from early man to speculation on man's future. Students were introduced chronologically to literary forms, with short stories and novels appearing later in the curriculum. At all times, there was emphasis on the basic conventions of standard English in oral and written composition. Areas such as music, fine arts and architecture were also incorporated into the curriculum content.

The mathematics program in the three-year curriculum consisted of instruction in the traditional areas—algebra, geometry, trigonometry, and pre-calculus. Computer math was also part of the program, since the language of the computer is now universal. Several enrichment topics such as the history of mathematics, the contributions of significant mathematicians, math in architecture and the arts, and the interpretation of statistics were included. A learning lab was established, not only for students in need of special assistance in the basic skills, but for highly motivated students who work well individually or in small groups.

Science, as with the other subjects, was chronologically integrated with the rest of the program. The emphasis was on the impact of science and technology on the nation and the world.

The emphasis for Spanish was on speaking and understanding the language as well as the cultures and national priorities of Hispanic countries.

In all three sequences, credit for community activities was granted.

Global education students could also choose other courses at Stevenson High as electives to fill in their six-hour day. This way, they kept in contact with friends in other parts of the school.

During the first three years, science was dropped due to lack of student interest and staff availability. Mathematics also proved to be difficult, due to the small number of students and large number of offerings. Only English, Spanish, and social studies are currently part of the instruction for the three-year global education curriculum. (note: the complete curriculum of the School of Global Education is outlined at the end of this chapter).

HELP FROM MANY QUARTERS

Leadership for the program was quickly assumed by Stevenson High's principal, Dr. Dale Coller, and by a teacher who became Director of the School of Global Education. (The Director is Dr. Jonathan Swift, author of this chapter.) They were greatly assisted by the rest of the faculty, and by the Parent Advisory Association.

Many people helped in preparing and implementing the curriculum. Chief among these were staff members from the Global Studies and the African Studies Centers at Michigan

State University who worked closely with the staff of the School of Global Education. Other educators from Michigan State, Wayne State University, and the University of Michigan, as well as consultants from the Wayne County Intermediate School District and the Livonia Public Schools District Curriculum Department, were also very helpful in the curriculum development phase. In addition, members of the Stevenson High Global Education Faculty Advisory Committee visited several alternative schools throughout the Midwest in 1977-78 to seek ideas and advice from others involved with alternative forms of education.

Through 1980, materials for the program were annually selected and purchased from Title 4-C grant funds. Since then, the Livonia Public Schools District has paid a proportionate student-population sum for texts and supplementary materials. There has been no shortage of funds for such purchases.

To support the program in the community, the Global Education Community Association was formed in 1978. The group's stated objectives included staff advisement, developing student opportunities, promoting relationships between all participants, raising community awareness of the project, and encouraging continuation and expansion of the program. This group has grown from less than 10 regular members to more than 100 today. Their accomplishments include a mayoral proclamation of "Livonia Global Awareness Day," sponsoring both local and overseas field trips, securing guest speakers, and both internal and external publicity and promotion. From time to time, parents attend classes or presentations by guest speakers. Teachers meet with parents often to keep them informed of both student progress and curricular activities.

PROBLEMS AND CONCERNS

During 1977-78, while members of the Faculty Advisory Board—including those teachers who ultimately were chosen to be the first teaching-team of the School of Global Education—were writing the unit plans and lessons for the new curriculum, discomfiture was increasing among the other 90 staff members of Stevenson High School. Although the project seemed to be a "done deal," many of their questions and concerns remained unanswered:

* What will be the student:teacher ratio in the project; will class sizes be a lot smaller than what the rest of us have to contend with?

* If the team is only 4-6 teachers, does this mean that students would have the same teachers for each subject for three years? Is this a good idea, either for the students or for the teachers?

* Is any teacher really competent to cover all of the courses in his/her subject that are planned for this curriculum?

* Will students be free to move in and out of the program over the three years?

* Will this program "skim off" our best students into the global education courses?

* Isn't a school-within-a-school going to create a lot of unnecessary problems and be a source of friction within the Stevenson faculty?

Part of the problem at this time was that the program had not yet won the official approval it needed from both the Board of Education and the State of Michigan. People who were involved in the planning stage could not talk openly about the details of the program, but had to talk in vague terms about "ideas" and "possibilities." As a result, rumors were rampant and many people were extremely angry at concepts they believed were in the program which in reality were not. Looking back from a vantage point of more than 12 years, it seems clear that many of the conflicts at the beginning could have been avoided if more care had been taken to introduce the project in a less threatening way.

As some of the veterans on the Stevenson High faculty had predicted, team teaching an integrated curriculum proved to be quite difficult. Several sources of friction surfaced between the global education team members, including interpersonal relations, emotional demands, differences in teaching style, and disagreements on issues such as field trips outside of school hours, sharing of duties and scheduling of teaching units. A workshop was held on team teaching but, in less than a year, all the workshop participants had left the program due to staff turnover and budget cuts.

ACCOMPLISHMENTS AND LEARNINGS

Even so, many positive elements emerged. As is common in alternative schools, relationships between the teachers and students in the program tended to be stronger than is usually true in the regular high school. Students felt comfortable in offering suggestions for improvement; for example, the values clarification unit was modified based on student reactions. The "family" pattern which was developed for the school enhanced the students' awareness of belonging, of being responsible for one's own actions; and of the right to fail or to make mistakes. The smaller, more supportive unit seemed to stimulate student initiative. Also, interdisciplinary work helped students to better understand the relationships of systems. It was also, they claimed, more interesting.

Much of the effectiveness of this curriculum, from the point of view of student interest and learning, depended on its experiential components. The concept of breaking down the walls of the classroom to let students out and of letting experts in was endorsed by alumni, students, parents, and teachers. The use of resource materials and group activities within the classroom has added to the program's success.

The global education syllabus, as written, is never covered completely. In a sense this is a reflection of the program's flexibility, one of the original goals of the project.

It is important to note that without the parent support group, many activities could not have been accomplished. Frequent meetings between teachers and parents over the years have built mutual trust and respect. These supportive parents tend to influence their own children, as well as their children's friends, to join the program. It was critical, in assembling the parent support group, to specify the goals of the association in such a way that there would be no sense of threat to the professional decision-making of teachers and administrators. This was accomplished quite successfully.

The School of Global Education is now well established at Stevenson High School, and continues to prosper. As awareness of global education spreads across the country, a correspondingly positive effect is felt in Livonia. There is considerable pride that the Stevenson program was one of the earliest programs in the nation. In the early years of the project, little was done to publicize the School of Global Education as a magnet school; now, that is being done. A series of cable television programs produced by "Globies," as the students call themselves, is helping to spread the word to the community.

Much has been learned by the School of Global Education staff. For example, while there may be some question about the role of the school principal as the key instructional leader, it is clear that without the principal's support, any innovative program can flounder. The principal can use both discretionary monies and influence to support programs which he believes to be worthwhile.

Also, before any program is considered for a school-within-a-school, adequate provision must be made for the staff of the regular school to have both communication and input in a structured and significant way.

Every method must be used to bring to the attention of the community all the pluses of the program in order to develop, as quickly as possible, positive public relations and community support.

In retrospect, it's significant to note that two types of fatalism became evident within the larger school staff: the antagonistic fatalism of the older, tenured teacher, and the paralyzing fatalism of the discouraged, "pink-slipped" teacher who didn't get involved because she could not be sure if she would be there the following September.

While the attitude and global philosophy of the teachers is of the utmost importance, they should be offered workshops which range from awareness of issues to skills to team-building and leadership, depending on the roles they are to assume. It is important to move to practical, day-to-day classroom management and instruction as soon as possible. Many of the worries of new teachers and those outside of the school were based on what they would be expected to do "differently" in the global education classroom. As much concern needs to be paid to ways to effect change as to the content itself. In addition to global studies, teachers need to be trained well in diagnosing needs, anticipating school environmental problems, and working with community members to initiate and maintain good public relations.

All global education teachers, regardless of discipline, need to get away from their own culture to experience one that is different. Otherwise, too much is vicarious experience which becomes third-hand when it reaches the students. Therefore, the travel component of the Livonia program takes on special significance.

It appears that in this type of program, team teaching is an advantage. This, however, requires willing teachers. Agreements must be made as a team, compromises must be worked out, decisions adhered to, and responsibilities shouldered as a group.

Certain people do seem to make better global education teachers than others. The qualities of humaneness, flexibility, humor, tolerance and fairness are qualities that identify most successful teachers, especially those who work well in alternative programs. Teachers who are sensitive and adept at varying instructional activities are likely to increase student enrollment. These teachers must be comfortable working closely as a team, while at the same time the team must maintain a certain amount of autonomy.

In a program which is trying to increase citizen participation, students should be included in curriculum decisions and in problem-solving. This increases their sense of belonging and ownership.

Particularly in multicultural studies, it is important to emphasize similarities rather than differences. If educators can help students learn that "different" does not imply either better or worse, they will help students adapt to the pluralistic society in which they live.

Beyond the initial implementation of the program and the cost in teacher time, such a project should cost no more than the regular school program. However, a strong parent support association can help produce additional funds for field trips and other activities.

Not enough testing was done to determine *affective* change, largely because no diagnosis was done at student entry. There does seem to be, however, clear and plentiful evidence of *cognitive* learning of global facts and concepts.

QUESTIONS AND RECOMMENDATIONS FOR THE FUTURE

As for the future, the teachers now working in the School of Global Education have suggested several questions for further investigation:

* Exactly what effect does the Model United Nations program have on the future of the participants?

* What kind of global education program can be developed which integrates both math and science?

* What influence does a community support group have on recruitment and retention patterns, absenteeism, the district office or the local principal?

* Are the reading selections of the volunteer global education students indicative of them as volunteers, or as global education students?

* Does a racially and ethnically integrated student body produce different behaviors, consistent with the goals of global education?

* How significant is travel experience, either in the United States or abroad, in the development of a global perspective? Does this depend on the country visited?

On the basis of their experiences, the Stevenson High School of Global Education made the following nine recommendations:

1. No program grants should be given by state agencies unless accompanied by a long-term commitment.

2. An agreement should be reached with the local teacher bargaining units, which will protect teachers assigned to the program.

3. Specific daily common preparation time or periodic released time should be given to team teaching members in order that they can work closely together on necessary planning and preparation.

4. University teams should be found to "adopt" the local global education project, supplying human and material resources and advice on evaluation and expansion of curricular activities.

5. Teacher training should be focused on the teachers' perceptions of their role, and on how their knowledge can be utilized in a new program.

6. While certain charismatic leaders can be important in initiating programs, it is recommended that local curriculum and leadership training organizations develop a cadre of backup teachers for both team and leadership positions.

7. A systematic research effort should be maintained by the teachers and administrators, to aid program review and determine priorities.

8. Every effort should be made to ensure a foreign language component in the global education program, preferably languages which are likely to be internationally important in the 21st century.

9. All high school exchange students automatically should be counseled into the global education program, to make it a microcosm of our increasingly pluralistic world.

*   *   *   *   *   *   *   *   *   *   *   *

THE SCHOOL OF GLOBAL EDUCATION

CURRICULUM

The School of Global Education offers a four-year curriculum in language arts, social sciences and foreign language open to any interested student who may wish to apply for enrollment.

Global education is a curriculum which will involve students in cultural, scientific, political and economic issues which affect everyone. In our school, it means an interdisciplinary curriculum offering English, social studies and foreign language in an arrangement different from what is offerd in the regular, larger school. Besides offering all the basic skills necessary for a career or university entrance, this alternative school promotes an understanding of the values and priorities of the many cultures of the world and of our American foreparents as well as the basic concepts and principles related to past and current world communities.

SEQUENCE 1-200

* English: Development of language, writing and communication (including writing and research skills), mythology, the beginnings of drama (all sequences include work in Humanities).

* Social Studies: Introduction to archeology, world history, sociology, georgraphy, anthropology, psychology, economics and political science.

SEQUENCE 2-201

* English: World and American literature, with the development of the novel, short story, poetry and drama (this will include writing skills and optional creative writing).

* Social Studies: American pluralism in history; native and immigrant trends; foreign policy.

SEQUENCE 3-202

* English: Contemporary world literature, trends and notable authors, new directions in drama, the novel, poetry, and non-fiction; science fiction and futurism (will include writing skills in research and rhetoric).

* Social Studies: Problems in global interdependence; studies in U.S. and comparative governments; major global issues; futurism.

SEQUENCE 4-203

* This one-semester, 1/2-credit course in debate is offered first semester. The objective is to prepare students in leadership and current United Nations topics, so that they may participate more actively in the Model United Nations.

SEQUENCE 5-203

* This 1/2-credit course is designed for those students who have already been introduced to beginning research techniques. It will entail a major research study of a global nature for either English or social studies credit under faculty guidance. It is expected that these students will use both community and university research facilities and will participate fully in the activities of the School of Global Education.

205-GLOBAL SPANISH 1

An introduction to spoken Spanish and the cultures of Hispanic countries. The course requires participating in speaking, reading and writing activities as well as projects and field trips. It lays the groundwork for a sensitivity to and understanding of how and why other nations and groups may be different.

206-GLOBAL SPANISH 2

A continuation of Global Spanish 1, this course emphasizes conversation together with an increased awareness of the concerns and cultures of Hispanic countries. It requires active participation in speaking, reading and writing activities as well as projects and field trips.

CHAPTER TWELVE

CONCLUSIONS

Kenneth A. Tye

There are a number of ways one might approach an examination of what happened at the various schools reported on in the previous chapters. The task could be done pragmatically, noting what worked in different schools and, at the same time, cataloging the various problems. This is pretty typical in American education. It leads to a prescription: a list of things to do to be successful (more often than not exactly ten).

We have been very slow to learn that this pragmatic approach to change in complex social systems such as schools is less than helpful. Think about how many how-to-do-it lists have been drawn up in your local school district in the past twenty years, for example.

A better way for us to come to grips with questions of educational change might be to amass a significant amount of descriptive data about practice and then begin to examine those data for patterns, relationships, and exceptions. Such examination can be deductive and/or inductive, without a priori conceptual lenses or with them. Rather than gaining how-to-do-it lists, we might gain understanding of a complex phenomenon, schooling.

It was in this spirit that this book was put together. Several case studies were solicited and written. It is the task of this chapter to examine those cases for patterns, relationships, and exceptions. To do this, the author has chosen to use a conceptual lense, that of the social movement.

The term, social movement, refers to a program or set of actions by a significant number of people directed toward a specific social change.[1] The United States began as a result of a revolution which was part of a worldwide social movement directed at overthrowing tyranny and at the establishment of democracy. Our history can be viewed as a series of social movements: Abolition, Secession, Temperance, Labor, Women's Rights, Populism, Civil Rights, McCarthyism, and Christian Fundamentalism, to name a few. Sometimes, social movements are in conflict with each other as currently is the case with the Pro-Life and Pro-Choice movements.

Five features of social movements seem to lend themselves to the examination of global education and, specifically, the school-based efforts described in this book. These are: (1) the conditions which produce the movement, (2) membership in the movement, (3) sociopolitical context, (4) structural properties, and (5) behaviors of the members.

THE CONDITIONS WHICH PRODUCE THE MOVEMENT

As was stated in the first chapter of this book and subsequently in several other chapters, most Americans are becoming aware of the growing economic, ecological, technological and even political and cultural interdependence of today's world. In terms of economics, we at least vaguely recognize the role played in our lives by multinational corporations, the negative balance of trade, and even the fact that the United States is once again a debtor nation. We understand that acid rain, nuclear fallout, oil spills, and waste management are global ecological problems. Satellite news broadcasts, fax machines, rapid air travel and the like demonstrate to us the international nature of modern technology. Events such as those in eastern

Europe with their concomitant effects upon local economies (e.g., closing of military bases, changing from jobs in the defense industry to ones in service or other peacetime industries) bring home to us the growing importance of global politics. Finally, most of us at least acknowledge the multicultural nature of today's society caused by the greatest period of human migration in recorded history. It is not uncommon to find over 50 languages spoken in large American high schools in "gateway" communities with significant immigrant populations.

It is these conditions which are producing the need for global education and it is the recognition of them which is causing growing support for the movement; and it seems safe to conclude that most, if not all, people who consider themselves to be global educators are attempting, in one way or another, to respond to such conditions. They have "joined" the global education "movement."

Impetus for joining this particular social movement probably only infrequently comes from within the schools themselves. In half of the cases reported on in this volume, school people specifically took on the task of globalizing the curriculum in response to a request to do so and a promise of resources from an outside agency. To be sure, many teachers understood, at least in part, changing world conditions and the need for a global perspective. However, it was the focus and resources provided by the outside agency which truly made concerted efforts possible.

Other reasons which caused people in these cases to turn to global education had nothing to do directly with the movement. In two schools, principals saw global education as a vehicle for making other curriculum changes—e.g., "overcoming an entrenched and tradition-bound curriculum." At least three schools saw it as a focus for a magnet school to meet pressures for desegregation. One school was responding to a state mandate for global education and another used it as part of an accountability plan. In some schools, more than one motivation was at work.

The importance to a movement such as global education of outside support agencies cannot be underestimated. In one case in this volume where there was no such agency, the project foundered badly. Teacher isolation, the many competing demands upon the time of teachers, and prevailing norms and traditions are just too strong to allow for a new movement such as global education to take hold at the earliest stages of its development without such support mechanisms.

It will be interesting to note what effect current world events have on the creation and support of such agencies. One could be led to hypothesize that these events are increasing the level of international consciousness in the population in general and that this increased consciousness, in turn, will result in increased political and financial support for the movement.

MEMBERSHIP IN THE MOVEMENT

The ultimate number of participants, particularly teachers, at the schools described in this book varied widely from just a few at one school to nearly all teachers at several others. Amounts and kinds of participation varied, also.

If this participation can in any way be seen as a measure of membership in the global education movement, then it seems appropriate to suggest four factors which are important to consider. These are: (1) initial expectations for membership, (2) level of administrative support, (3) amount and kinds of resources available, and (4) culture of the school.

In the schools described in this book where a large number of teachers ultimately participated, it appeared that the expectation from the very beginning was that all or as many as possible of the faculty were to be involved. On the other hand, where a specific "team" was identified initially as having ownership, recruitment of further members was very difficult or impossible. This suggests that, right from the beginning of a project, the expectation should be built that the movement is directed toward all or most of the faculty. It also suggests that the "infusion" model may be more successful in facilitating the movement than a model which calls for specific global education courses.2 This certainly is consistent with the literature on how social movements grow.

Administrative support, particularly that of the principal, seemed critical to getting a good start in the schools under discussion. In a couple of cases, formal leaders "got on the bandwagon" only after there was positive recognition by some outside source(s). They were "for" the particular global education program once it got good publicity. This is not surprising. Frequently, when the impetus for a new idea comes from people other than the formal leaders, they need to be convinced of its merits.

Administrative support, alone, was not enough to cause the spread of global education in this sample of schools. To be sure, it helped. However, there were schools where the principals and other administrators were positive but where only a few teacher really ever became involved or where teachers participated only at a minimum level. In one case, after a supportive principal was transferred, teachers attempted to withdraw from the new global education emphasis and return to the traditional program which had existed previously.

Almost all of the schools discussed here had extra resources available to them in the form of grants, staff development, release time, consultants, materials, and the like. Such resources were important and, in fact, toward the end, some of the projects were perceived as being in danger because special funding was being withdrawn. It is probably true that the future growth of global education will be slowed if special resources are not available. It also is probably true that many of the teachers who have been involved will continue to bring a global perspective to what they do whether or not special resources remain available.

Clear initial expectations, supportive leadership and sufficient resources all seem helpful to the growth of a social movement such as global education. However, from the experiences described here, what seems even more important in determining growth of membership in the movement is the culture of the school. This is a complex concept, but is at the heart of the change process.

In several of these schools, as is the case in many others where there is an attempt to create new programs, there were teachers who were seen as resistant to change, specifically to global education. This is a bit unfair. They were not necessarily resistant. Rather, they were "for" that which was traditional and generally accepted. They subscribed to the established norms. Herein lies the major work of the change agent, the advocate of any given social movement. We shall return to this notion toward the end of this chapter.

Before leaving the topic of membership in the global education movement, four further brief observations should be made. First, in all of the cases represented here, there were people involved from two or more disciplines. Global education, as demonstrated in these schools, is inter-disciplinary.

Second, and while the majority of global education programs in the United States are at the high school level, there are a number of successful efforts at the elementary and middle school levels. That was true in this sample, as well.

Third, there has been some criticism of global education in the past because it has tended, at times, to be organized to serve only academically advanced students and/or students from upper socioeconomic groups. A number of the schools described here showed that this does not have to be the case. Global education is for all students.

Finally, and while it was not discussed much in these cases, there was some evidence that many of the global education agencies and/or schools also collaborated with other agencies such as Educators for Social Responsibility, the United Nations Association and the Geography Alliance when it was appropriate. This seems a good thing and is mentioned only because there is a misguided tendency in some global education circles to be possessive about the movement. The fact is that advocates of a social movement, in order to be successful, probably need to make alliances with a variety of like minded people. Networking of all kinds has been show to be a powerful change strategy.

SOCIOPOLITICAL CONTEXT

It is interesting to note, with all of the publicity which has accrued to the political controversy surrounding some global education projects in the nation, that none of the authors in this volume pointed to serious problems at the schools they described. Some schools did call their projects "international education" or "multicultural education" rather than global education as a way of avoiding controversy. A couple of schools very wisely formed community and/or parent advisory groups which helped to legitimatize their programs. Some projects were legitimate because they were part of a choice (magnet school) program. One school was responding to a state law mandating global education.

All of the schools reported on in this volume were careful to explain their programs to the public. This is critical for any social movement such as global education because it calls for a major change in thinking and it has to do with deeply held values. Lack of explanation can lead to serious misinterpretations.

Two groups are particularly threatened by global education. The first group, mostly comprised of religious fundamentalists, see it as a manifestation of secular humanism which threatens their deeply held religious beliefs. The other group is made up of individuals and sub-groups, often interlocking, who see global education as a threat to the promotion and dominance of American ideals throughout the world. The fact that global education seeks to promote a realistic view of the world and the ongoing changes in the cultural, ecological, economic, political land technological systems therein is lost on both groups.

What proponents of global education must do, as many of the people in these schools did, is to be proactive about the movement: create a rationale, enlist community support, continually explain what is being done, engage people in discussions about world conditions and what these mean for them and their children, cite societal leaders who advocate the movement, and point out accomplishments.

Further, global educators need to use good professional judgement and common sense. For example, examining all sides of controversial issues is important and justifiable. Being an advocate for a single position is not. Likewise, maintaining a scholarly outlook and avoiding sentimentality is advisable. In that regard, it should be noted that most schools described in this volume had connections to one or more sources of funded knowledge—e.g., universities, museums, centers.

Finally, it is important to recognize that support for global education is growing within the general body politic. The projects reported on here were pioneering efforts, toward the beginning of what is being called a social movement. World events, shifting perceptions and the efforts of such early programs are causing more and more people to see the need for global education. It is the hope of the authors of this book that others can learn from the successes and problems encountered in these early programs.

STRUCTURAL PROPERTIES

A number of structural matters have already been discussed here and will not be gone over again in depth. It is sufficient to remind the reader of just a couple of things. First, the cases presented in this volume clearly point to the importance of sanction and support from those in leadership positions and from the superordinate system. That is quite different than mandates, however. What is being suggested by these programs is not that teacher be directed to globalize their curricula. Rather, what these pioneer programs demonstrate is the importance of teachers exercising their professional roles and administrators making this possible.[3]

Second, the importance of linkages of teachers to funded knowledge has also been demonstrated by the cases reported here. The legitimatizing role of knowledge centers has already been pointed out. Also, it is unrealistic to assume that teachers are expert about all or even many aspects of global systems (cultural, ecological, economic, political, technological), and in-service opportunities to give them appropriate knowledge are imperative. Of course, time needs to be provided for such activity.

It cannot be assumed, either, that teachers are expert in all aspects of pedagogy. One of the things which these cases at least hint at is the need to break away from total reliance upon textbooks and frontal teaching. Global education lends itself well to such teaching-learning strategies as community surveys, simulation, cooperative learning, construction, cooking and artistic performance.

One of the problems associated with in-service education in the past has been the tendency for it to have an individual rather than school focus. That is, individual teachers have tended to go off to college courses, district or intermediate agency workshops and then return to their classrooms wherein they have applied their often quite good learning to their own teaching. There has tended to be little in-service focused upon groups of teachers or entire faculties. There was some group focused in-service in the schools described in this volume and it is hypothesized that such a focus is more effective in bringing about overall school improvement.

The question of why, in some schools, many teachers did not participate in global education activities has already been addressed. One thing which has not been pointed out and which is extremely significant is that teachers frequently just don't perceive that they have time for anything new in their curriculum, particularly if it is viewed as something with which they lack familiarity. Part of the problem in these schools was that global education was seen as an "add on," something to be attached to the current curriculum rather than as a different perspective on what was already being taught. Part was that inadequate resources for such things as release time and materials were available. Mainly, teachers simply felt that they had too many things to do already. "Time" was seen as the major obstacle to the implementation of global education. Whether it truly was or not is probably debatable for time is a commodity which can be reorganized. On the other hand, there is no doubt that today's teachers are caught up in competing demands upon their time.

Many of the projects reported on here relied on teams of teachers working together. In some cases, it was just that team arrangement which ultimately got in the way. Teaming *is* a desirable structural arrangement. However, it cannot be assumed that people can work together in a team simply because they have a common interest, in this case globalizing the curriculum. Culturally, Americans are highly individualistic and there is no reason to assume that it should be any different in our schools. Teacher isolation has been the norm because we have created structures to promote it: separate classrooms, "houses," and the like. People have to learn how to plan, teach and evaluate together. It doesn't just happen.

In at least two of the schools described in this book, the matter of defining global education was raised. Many global educators contend that such definitions, agreed upon by participants, are crucial because they determine purpose and content as well as allow for clear communication within the school, with policy makers and with the lay public.

On the other hand, there are a number of people, this author included, who contend that preoccupation with definition early in a social movement such as global education can be detrimental. It can be hypothesized that people can begin a project by carrying out *activity* based upon whatever meaning global education has for them individually at the time. As they proceed through activity and as they interact with others engaged in similar activity, meaning changes and definitions are formulated which are far richer and which are less apt to be narrow and restrictive. Such an approach should be a conscious one which allows the necessary time for reflection and discussion. The idea of creating emergent meanings should not be confused with "muddling through," however.

BEHAVIORS OF THE MEMBERS

Earlier in this chapter there was a brief discussion of the apparent resistance to global education on the part of a number of teachers. It was pointed out that this is somewhat unfair because, looked at from another perspective, they were actually "for" something they considered to be "traditional."

Educational change strategies can be classified into four general categories. Probably the most commonly observed strategies are those which can be labelled "political." These have to do with setting policy, always involve the accumulation and use of authority and power, and, almost inevitably, lead to conflict. In schooling, the current common manifestation of political strategies is the mandating of curriculum, administrative arrangements, time, and the like by state authorities. In this book, there were reports from a few schools which were in states which had mandated global education. Other mandates, state or federal, which had an effect upon these schools included those for desegregation, testing and other forms of accountability.

Political strategies, since they involve the use of authority, are used at other levels of the system, also. The roles played by some district administrators and principals in initiating or impeding global education efforts in the schools discussed in this book were often political, particularly when teachers were directed to behave in certain ways.

As was pointed out earlier, mandates can serve to legitimatize change efforts. They did in some of the schools described here. On the other hand, they never, by themselves, seem to actually change basic classroom practice.

We also see a lot of "technical" change strategies. These have to do with altering the technology of the field. The introduction of computers and teaching machines is an obvious example, but the training of teachers in new content and/or teaching methods is even more common. Much of what occurred in the case studies can be classified here. Technical strategies are important and, in many instances, necessary. As is the case with political strategies, however, they are not enough, by themselves, to create significant change at the school level.

"Structural" change strategies are ones we seem to be most attracted to. Perhaps that is because they appear to be easier to carry out. However, as with other kinds of change strategies, without accompanying changes in behavior, they tend not to be very productive. Implementing a student advisory program serves as a good example. If a homeroom period is created and used only for announcements and study hall, little, if anything, is changed for students. On the other hand, when teachers in such programs are trained to be able to assist students with academic, career, and/or personal matters, advisory can make a difference. The point is, the changing of the schedule (a structure) to include an advisory period has to be accompanied by a change in teacher behavior.

Changing time schedules, reorganizing line and staff relationships, refiguring who works with whom, changing grade level patterns (e.g., K-8 to K-5, 6-8) are kinds of structural changes in education. The formation of interdisciplinary teams and the creation of a school-within-a-school program are examples of structural changes in the cases in this book. On reflection, the question of how successful each one was seems to relate to how much change in behavior also occurred.

What is called for, in addition to political, technical and/or structural changes which can *facilitiate* the work of the school is what organization development people refer to as "behavioral" change.[4] This means that people actually learn to behave in different ways toward each other: administrators to teachers, teachers to teachers, teachers to students, and so on. Such things as clear communication, shared leadership and decision-making, healthy conflict resolution, and thoughtful problem solving are learned and practiced in an open and trusting environment.

We have known for several decades now that the kind of organization development briefly described here is what is really needed to change the cultures of our schools (not to mention businesses, hospitals, etc.) but we don't seem to be willing or able to commit ourselves to pursue such goals. Global education is a social movement that is concerned with cross system understanding and perspective taking. It is ideal as a vehicle for bringing about cultural change in our schools if it is viewed in conjunction with behaviors of the members of the organization. This is not a radical idea. It grows naturally out of the pioneering work of people such as those in the schools described in this volume.

NOTES

1. Joseph Gusfield. *Protest, Reform and Revolt: A Reader in Social Movements.* New York: John Wiley & Sons, 1970.

2. Toni Kirkwood, in Chapter Ten, described the Robert Hanvey work which serves many projects as the rationaled for "infusion" of a global perspective into all subject areas.

3. The author refuses to use the term "empower" teachers although it is quite the popular thing to do these days. Empowerment implies malefic generosity. It is *not* the role of administrators to "give" power to teachers (or take it

away). Administrators have the job of facilitating the work of professional teachers—e.g., provision of time, material, psychological support. Perhaps hospital administration is a good example.

4. See, for example, Donald F. Harvey and Donald R. Brown. *An Experiential Approach To Organization Development* (3rd ed.), Englewood Cliffs, N.J.: Prentice-Hall, 1988. These authors discuss structural, technical, and behavioral organization change strategies.

ABOUT THE AUTHORS

David Gidich is principal of the Northeast "International Studies" magnet school, Montclair, New Jersey. He is completing his doctoral studies in school administration at Teachers College, Columbia University.

Gary Howard is the founder and executive director of the REACH Center for Multicultural and Global Education (Respecting Ethnic and Cultural Heritage). The center is a non-profit organization providing multicultural/global training and curriculum to schools and businesses throughout the United States.

Toni Fuss-Kirkwood is a global educator and coordinates the international/global education program, Dade County Public Schools, Miami, Florida.

Dennis Lubeck directs the International Education Consortium (IEC) in St. Louis. He was a high school history teacher for 20 years prior to receiving his Ph.D. in American Studies. He also serves as adjunct professor of education at Washington University.

Paul Mulloy has been a social studies teacher at Winchester, Massachusetts high schools since 1970 and Director of the Massachusetts Global Education Project (MGEP) since 1979. He is co-author of *Global Issues Activities and*

Resources for High School Teachers and *Massachusetts in the World, An Activity and Resource Book.*

Kathy O'Neill, a former staff associate at the Center for Human Interdependence, holds an MA in Latin American Studies and a BA in secondary education. Her interest in cross-cultural issues led her to language teaching in the U.S. and abroad; bilingual education; and administering international cultural exchanges and language acquisition programs.

George Otero is a founder and currently Chairman of the Board of Las Palomas de Taos, a non-profit Global Education learning center and conference facility located in the historic Mabel Dodge Luhan home. Formerly, he spent four years at the University of Denver's Center for Teaching International Relations.

Terry Reger is the K-12 Social Science Studies Coordinator for the Ferguson-Florissant School District. She serves on the NCATE Board of Examiners and publishes curriculum on China with Dr. George Hatch from Washington University. She won the Outstanding Secondary Teacher of Social Science in Missouri Award in 1985.

Jennifer Schumaker is a human ecologist, from South Africa and currently living in Arkansas. She works in international agricultural development for Heifer Project International.

Jonathan Swift is the director of the pioneer School of Global Education in Livonia, Michigan. A doctoral graduate of Michigan State in curriculum, he is also a member of the International/Global Education Steering Committee of the Association for Supervision and Curriculum Development.

Kenneth A. Tye is Co-director of the Center for Human Interdependence (CHI). He is also on the faculty at Chapman College in Orange, Califonia. He is editor of *Global Education: From Thought to Action* and co-author of *Global Education: A Study of School Change*.

Ida Urso was a staff associate at CHI. She has taught courses at various universities in global education, human rights in the world community, and comparative education. She is founder and chairperson of the non-profit Center for Planetary Goodwill.